Sixtieth-Anniversary Edition

The Museum of Modern Art, New York

Distributed by Harry N. Abrams, Inc., New York

Machine Art

March 6 to April 30, 1934

The Museum of Modern Art, New York

The Sixtieth-Anniversary Edition of *Machine Art* is made possible by a generous grant from Jo Carole and Ronald S. Lauder.

Note to the Sixtieth-Anniversary Edition: The preceding title page and the pages immediately following the Preface to the Sixtieth-Anniversary Edition (on page 5) are facsimiles of the original, 1934 edition of *Machine Art*. On the last page of the book, formerly blank, is a current listing of the Museum's Trustees and Committee on Architecture and Design.

Copyright © 1934 by The Museum of Modern Art, New York
Reprint edition, 1969, Arno Press
Sixtieth-Anniversary Edition copyright © 1994 by The Museum of Modern Art, New York
All rights reserved.

Library of Congress Catalogue Card Number: 94-74587
ISBN: 0-87070-135-5 (MoMA; T&H)
ISBN: 0-8109-6150-4 (Abrams)
Printed by Hull Printing, Meriden, Connecticut
Bound by Mueller Trade Bindery, Middletown, Connecticut
Published by
The Museum of Modern Art
11 West 53 Street
New York, New York 10019

Distributed in the United States and Canada by Harry N. Abrams, Inc., New York, A Times Mirror Company

Distributed outside the United States and Canada by Thames & Hudson, Ltd., London

Printed in the United States of America

Preface to the Sixtieth-Anniversary Edition

Sixty years later, the *Machine Art* exhibition naturally seems dated. In 1934 we were in our twenties. Adrenalin was running high; machine worship was running wild. After all, the influence of Marinetti's machine-crazed Futurist movement was not so long before.

How much has changed! Chaos theory has replaced classic certainties. We prefer Heraclitan flux to Platonic ideas, the principle of uncertainty to the model of perfection, complexity to simplicity.

My catalogue text seems juvenile today, with its quick, unsubstantiated judgments thrown around and conclusions reached without documentation or research. Nevertheless, the thrust was clear: anti-handicraft, industrial methods alone satisfied our age; Platonic dreams of perfection were the ideal. Complexity and uncertainty were not the aim of the 1934 show. It was a piece of propaganda by the great preacher and proselytizer for modern art Alfred Barr. I was his willing acolyte.

Today I find that the best designs in the exhibition and catalogue were not the elegantly simple ones, such as the petri dishes and beakers, but the exceptional, "artistic" ones. I could name three: first, the cover of the catalogue itself, designed by the Bauhaus artist Josef Albers, and then the Whitworth drill press of the mid-nineteenth century and the Art Nouveau bowl by the Belgian designer Henry Van de Velde (catalogue figures b and c). I admit that I could, however immodestly, add a fourth: my installation design, which is obviously not in the original catalogue but is reproduced on the following page for the anniversary edition.

Installation view of *Machine Art*, 1934

By the end of the thirties the aesthetic of the machine had been rapidly absorbed into the design movements of the time, and needs no further historical mention. More interesting is the later story, the development of the "moderne," the French Art Deco, and the neoclassical. Sixty years ago our horizon was bounded by Piet Mondrian, the Bauhaus, Le Corbusier, and Mies van der Rohe. Since then Neo-Expressionism, Deconstructivism, and historicism all have flourished.

The narrow channeling of the arts of design and architecture that we predicted has broken out into a pluralist flood. And we enjoy it all!

Philip Johnson
New York City
December 1994

LENDERS TO THE EXHIBITION

The Accessories Co., Inc., 40 West 40th Street, N. Y.
                                        Division American Radiator Co.
    Bathroom equipment

Aluminum Company of America, Pittsburgh, Pa.
    Tubing, pistons, propellers, radiators, partitions

The Aluminum Cooking Utensil Co., New Kensington, Pa.

American Radiator Co., 40 West 40th Street, N. Y.

American Sheet & Tin Plate Co., 71 Broadway, N. Y.
                                        Subsidiary United States Steel Corp.

    Stainless steel partitions, automobile hubcap

American Steel & Wire Co., Worcester, Mass.   Subsidiary United States Steel Corp.
    Cables, springs, strip steel

Arundell Clarke Ltd., 620 Fifth Avenue, N. Y.
    Ash tray

The Bingham Stamping & Tool Co., 1062 Post Street, Toledo, Ohio
                                        (R. Aberli, Jr., 225 Fifth Avenue, N. Y.)
    Trays

Bissell Carpet Sweeper Co., Grand Rapids, Mich. (46 West Broadway, N. Y.)

The Brown Instrument Co., Philadelphia, Pa.
    Meter

Brown & Sharpe Manufacturing Co., Providence, R. I.
                                        (Brown & Sharpe of N. Y., Inc., 20 Vesey Street, N. Y.)
    Precision instruments

L. D. Cahn Co., 81 Spring Street, N. Y.
    Stainless steel utensils

Carnegie Steel Co., Pittsburgh, Pa.   Subsidiary United States Steel Corp.
    Car wheel and axle

Chase Brass & Copper Co., Waterbury, Conn.
                                        (Specialty Sales Division, 200 Fifth Avenue, N. Y.)
    Bowls, trays, plates

Clyde-Mallory Line
    Switchboard

Conant Bros. Co., Somerville, Mass., (6 East 45th Street, N. Y.)
    Bathroom fittings

The Conover Co., Chicago, Ill., (101 Park Avenue, N. Y.)
    Dishwasher

Coors Porcelain Co., Golden, Colorado
    Laboratory porcelain

P. & F. Corbin, 101 Park Avenue, N. Y.
  Hardware

Corning Glass Works, Corning, N. Y., (501 Fifth Avenue, N. Y.)
  Laboratory glass, vases, bowls

Design Engineers, Inc., 745 Fifth Avenue, N. Y.
  Picture frames

Dictaphone Sales Corporation, 420 Lexington Avenue, N. Y.

Eugene Dietzgen Co., Inc., 218 East 23rd Street, N. Y.
  Drafting and surveying instruments

Henry Disston & Sons, Inc., Philadelphia, Pa.
  Saw, trowel

Distillers Products Corp., Empire State Building, N. Y.
  Rumidor

Alfred Dunhill of London, Inc., 622 Fifth Avenue, N. Y.
  Pipes and smoking accessories

Eimer & Amend, Third Avenue at 18th Street, N. Y.
  Laboratory glass, scientific instruments

Electric Boat Company, Bayonne, N. J.
  Propeller

Electrol Inc., 227 East 45th Street, N. Y.
  Furnace

Electromaster Inc., 1803 East Atwater Street, Detroit, Mich.
  Range

The Fay Co., 130 Madison Avenue, N. Y.
  Floor machine

Fleetwings, Inc., Garden City, L. I.
  Aeroplane wing rib

Ford Motor Co., Dearborn, Mich.
  Headlamps

Ford Motor Co., Dearborn, Mich.   (Louis C. Eitzen, 280 Broadway, N. Y.)
  Measuring device

Fostoria Glass Co., Moundsville, W. Va., (200 Fifth Avenue, N. Y.)
  Tumblers, goblets, plates, vases

The Gorham Co., Providence, R. I., (6 West 48th Street, N. Y.)
  Flat silver

Hamilton Beach Manufacturing Co., Racine, Wis.   (280 Broadway, N. Y.)
  Vacuum cleaner

Hamilton-Standard Propeller Corp., Hartford, Conn.

LENDERS TO THE EXHIBITION—Continued

Hanson Scale Co., 523 North Ada Street, Chicago, Ill., (1150 Broadway, N. Y.)
  Bathroom scale

Hoffmann & Billings Manufacturing Co., Milwaukee, Wis.
                                      (Henry Stein, 50 Cliff Street, N. Y.)
  Mixer Faucet

Holophane Co., Inc., 342 Madison Avenue, N. Y.
  Diffusing lenses

Howell Co., Geneva, Ill.
  Metal chairs

The International Nickel Co., Inc., 67 Wall Street, N. Y.
  Sink

Jaeger Watch Co., Inc., 304 East 45th Street, N. Y.

Janes & Kirtland, Inc., 101 Park Avenue, N. Y.
  Kitchen cabinets

Lalance & Grosjean Mfg. Co., Woodhaven, L. I. (405 Lexington Avenue, N. Y.)
  Kitchenware

Leeds & Northrup Co., 4901 Stenton Avenue, Philadelphia, Pa.
  Potentiometer

Lenox Inc., Trenton, N. J.
  Porcelain vases, plates

Lewis & Conger, 45th Street and Sixth Avenue, N. Y.
  Knives, spoons, enamel kitchenware, glassware

Lily-Tulip Cup Corp., 122 East 42nd Street, N. Y.
  Paper cups and containers, dispensers

Herman Miller Clock Co., Zeeland, Mich. (62 West 47th Street, N. Y.)

The National Cash Register Co., Dayton, Ohio. (205 East 42nd Street, N. Y.)

National Tube Co., Pittsburgh, Pa. Subsidiary United States Steel Corp.
  Stainless steel tubing

Ovington's, Fifth Avenue at 39th Street, N. Y.
  Imported glassware, enlarging mirror

Owens-Illinois Glass Co., Toledo, Ohio. (405 Lexington Avenue, N. Y.)
  Bottles and jars

Platinel, Inc., 103 Washington Avenue, Albany, N. Y.
  Ash tray

Platinum Products Co., 521 Fifth Avenue, N. Y.
  Cigarette lighters

Polar Ware Co., Inc., Sheboygan, Wis. (239 Eleventh Avenue, N. Y.)
  Kitchenware

Revere Copper & Brass Inc., Rome Manufacturing Division, Rome, N. Y.
                                      (230 Park Avenue, N. Y.)
  Kitchenware, bowls

Ritter Dental Manufacturing Co., Inc., Rochester, N. Y. (200 Fifth Avenue, N. Y.)
  X-ray apparatus

S K F Industries, Inc., Front Street and Erie Avenue, Philadelphia, Pa.
  Ball bearing

Saks-Fifth Avenue, 611 Fifth Avenue, N. Y.
  Accessories

Scovill Manufacturing Co., Waterville, Conn.
  Flush valve

Scully Steel Products Co., Waverly, N. J. Subsidiary United States Steel Corp.
  Rolled steel sections

The Silex Company, Hartford, Conn. (E. B. Latham & Co., 250 Fourth Ave., N. Y.)

Standard Gage Co., Poughkeepsie, N. Y. Subsidiary Ford Motor Co.
                                   (Louis C. Eitzen, 280 Broadway, N. Y.)
  Measuring device

The Standard Oil Co. of Ohio, Cleveland, Ohio
  Gasoline pump

Carol Stupell, 443 Madison Avenue, N. Y.
  Martini mixer

Sullivan Shipyards, Inc., 827 East 9th Street, N. Y.
  Propeller

Taylor Instrument Companies, Rochester, N. Y. (30 Rockefeller Plaza, N. Y.)

Thonet Brothers, Inc., 33 East 47th Street, N. Y.
  Metal chairs

The Torsion Balance Co., 92 Reade Street, N. Y.
  Torsion scale

United States Steel Corp., 71 Broadway, New York—Lent through subsidiaries

Kurt Versen, 19 East 47th Street, N. Y.
  Lighting fixtures

Waters-Genter Co., Minneapolis, Minn.
                  (Tumbridge Sales Corp., 196 Lexington Avenue, N. Y.)
  Electrical cooking appliances

Western Clock Co., LaSalle, Ill.

Westinghouse Electric & Manufacturing Co., N. Y.
  Insulators, lamps, fuse, switchboard, micarta panels, meters, clock motors

The S. S. White Dental Manufacturing Co., 500 Fifth Avenue, N. Y.

Russel Wright, 165 East 35th Street, N. Y.
  Wooden bowls and tableware

The Yale & Towne Manufacturing Co., Stamford, Conn.
  Padlock

York Safe & Lock Co., York, Pa. (55 Maiden Lane, N. Y.)

Carl Zeiss Inc., 485 Fifth Avenue, N. Y.
  Optical instruments

In addition to those who have lent to the Exhibition, the President and Trustees of The Museum of Modern Art wish to thank
for their assistance in procuring objects not manufactured or owned by them

> United States Steel Corporation
> Westinghouse Electric & Manufacturing Company
> Aluminum Company of America

for generously lending materials for installation

> American Sheet & Tin Plate Company, Subsidiary United States Steel Corp.
> Aluminum Company of America
> Westinghouse Electric & Manufacturing Company
> Lily-Tulip Cup Corporation

for the design of the cover

> Prof. Josef Albers, Black Mountain College, Black Mountain, N. C.

for the photography in the catalog

> Miss Ruth Bernhard

for his assistance in designing the installation

> Mr. Jan von Ruhtenberg, of Stockholm

for their special advice

> Prof. C. R. Richards, of the New York Museum of Science & Industry
> Prof. H. R. Hitchcock, Jr. of Wesleyan University

σχημάτων τε γὰρ κάλλος οὐχ ὅπερ ἂν ὑπολάβοιεν οἱ πολλοὶ πειρῶμαι νῦν λέγειν, ἢ ζῴων ἤ τινων ζωγραφημάτων, ἀλλ᾽ εὐθύ τι λέγω, φησὶν ὁ λόγος, καὶ περιφερὲς καὶ ἀπὸ τού- των δὴ τά τε τοῖς τόρνοις γιγνόμενα ἐπίπεδά τε καὶ στερεὰ καὶ τὰ τοῖς κανόσι καὶ γωνί- αις, εἴ μου μανθάνεις. ταῦτα γὰρ οὐκ εἶναι πρός τι καλὰ λέγω, καθάπερ ἄλλα, ἀλλ᾽ ἀεὶ καλὰ καθ᾽ αὑτὰ πεφυκέναι . . .

By beauty of shapes I do not mean, as most people would suppose, the beauty of living figures or of pictures, but, to make my point clear, I mean straight lines and circles, and shapes, plane or solid, made from them by lathe, ruler and square. These are not, like other things, beautiful relatively, but always and absolutely.

Plato: *Philebus* 51 c

Ad pulchritudinem tria requiruntur. Primo quidem integritas, sive per- fectio: quae enim diminuta sunt, hoc ipso turpia sunt. Et debita proportio, sive consonantia. Et iterum claritas: unde quae habent colorem nitidum, pulchra esse dicuntur.

For beauty three things are required. First, then, integrity or per- fection: those things which are broken are bad for this very reason. And also a due proportion or harmony. And again clarity: whence those things which have a shining color are called beautiful.

**St. Thomas Aquinas: *Summa Theologiae*, I, q. 39, a. 8.,
quoted by Jacques Maritain in *Art et Scolastique*,
Paris, 1927, page 250**

Industrial civilization must either find a means of ending the divorce between its industry and its "culture" or perish.

L. P. Jacks: *Responsibility and Culture*

FOREWORD

Machine Art and Geometrical Beauty.

The beauty of machine art is in part the abstract beauty of "straight lines and circles" made into actual tangible "surfaces and solids" by means of tools, "lathes and rulers and squares." In Plato's day the tools were simple handworker's implements but today, as a result of the perfection of modern materials and the precision of modern instruments, the modern machine-made object approaches far more closely and more frequently those pure shapes the contemplation of which Plato calls the first of the "pure pleasures."

Machines are, visually speaking, a practical application of geometry. Forces which act in straight lines are changed in direction and degree by machines which are themselves formed of straight lines and curves. The lever is geometrically a straight line resting on a point. The wheel and axle is composed of concentric circles and radiating straight lines. The watch spring (No. 7) is a spiral. Sphericity and circularity are the geometrical characteristics of a ball bearing (No. 50). Screws, bearing springs (No. 1), and propellers (No. 41) are various—and variously beautiful—applications of the helix and helicoid.

Static and Kinetic Rhythms.

The beauty of machine art depends often upon rhythmical as well as upon geometrical elements—upon repetition as well as upon shape. The teeth of a saw form a simple static rhythmic series; the keys and levers of the cash register (No. 88) make a more varied and complex series.

Motion is an essential function of many machines and sometimes increases their aesthetic interest, principally through the addition of temporal rhythms, both of movement and of sound. The pistons of a locomotive or the rising and falling frames of a mechanical loom illustrate the point. On the other hand a propeller, a governor, a rotary saw, a ball bearing are more beautiful as objects when they are still or, better, moving very slowly. Even the streamlined object is more frequently admired when at rest than when in motion. Fortunately for this exhibition machines proper are only a small part of machine art as a whole.

Technical and Material Beauty.

In addition to perfection of shape and rhythm, beauty of surface is an important aesthetic quality of machine art at its best. Perfection of surface is, of course, made possible by the refinement of modern materials and the precision of machine manufacture. A watch spring is beautiful not only for its spiral shape but also for its bright steel surface and its delicately exact execution.

Machine art, devoid as it should be of surface ornament, must depend upon the sensuous beauty of porcelain, enamel, celluloid, glass of all colors, copper, aluminum, brass and steel. The circles and spheres of a ball bearing (No. 50) are greatly enhanced by the contrasting surfaces of brushed steel races, shining polished steel balls, and brass carriers.

Visual Complexity.

The beauty in machine art as in all art varies in relation but not in proportion to its complexity. A watch crystal, perfect though it may be, is too simple a form to hold our visual interest for long. A printing press, on the other hand, is too complicated an arrangement of shapes for the human eye to enjoy aesthetically. Moderately simple machine compositions such as the door of a wall safe (No. 91) or the microscope (No. 314) or our classical example, the ball bearing (No. 50) prove more satisfactory.

Function.

A knowledge of function may be of considerable importance in the visual enjoyment of machine art, though Plato might have considered such knowledge an impurity. Mechanical function and utilitarian function—"how it works" and "what it does"—are distinct problems, the former requiring in many cases a certain understanding of mechanics, the latter, of practical use. Whoever understands the dynamics of pitch in propeller blades (No. 41) or the distribution of forces in a ball bearing (No. 50) so that he can participate imaginatively in the action of mechanical functions is likely to find that this knowledge enhances the beauty of the objects.* In the same way, using or understanding the use of, the calipers (No. 294), the retort (No. 394), or the rotary floor polisher (No. 71) is likely to increase their aesthetic value.

* For most people the beauty of that ingenious engine, the Gothic vault, is augmented by a knowledge of the mechanics which govern its structure and visible form.

Fortunately the functional beauty of most of the objects is not obscure and in any case, so far as this exhibition is concerned, appreciation of their beauty in the platonic sense is more important.

Machine Art and the Designer.

The previous paragraphs have considered the aesthetic enjoyment of machines and machine-made objects without mentioning their designers. The designers are of two kinds, technical and artistic. Often one man will combine both rôles. For even the most impractical and fantastic "styler" of "modernistic" plumbing fixtures (not included in the exhibition) must consider function; and the most forthright technical designer of microscopes (No. 314) will insist on a perfection of shape and finish which is partially aesthetic.

Many of the finest objects in the exhibition such as the bearing spring (No. 1) or the depth gauge (No. 289) are produced quite without benefit of artist-designer. Their beauty is entirely unintentional—it is a by-product. Nevertheless they satisfy through their "integrity", "due proportion" and "clarity," the excellent thomistic definition of the beautiful as "that which being seen, pleases".*

Many other objects, the clock (No. 270), the chair (No. 282), the lamp (No. 273), are the result of conscious artistic intention. For in a great many useful objects function does not *dictate* form, it merely indicates form in a general way. The rôle of the artist in machine art is to choose, from a variety of possible forms each of which may be functionally adequate, that one form which is aesthetically most satisfactory. He does not embellish or elaborate, but refines, simplifies and perfects.

Machine Art and Fine Art.

Good machine art is entirely independent of painting, sculpture and architecture. But it may be noted in passing that modern artists have been much influenced by machine art. The Italian futurists, Russolo and Balla, and their English and Russian followers were romantically excited by the power and speed—the *dinamismo*—of machines.† Painters such as Léger and Baumeister have been interested in the decorative and formal qualities

* *Id quod visum placet;* Saint Thomas Aquinas—*Summa Theologiae* I, g. 5, a 4, ad 1.

† The romantic attitude toward the machine reached its height in America about five years ago. The Machine-Age Exhibition held in New York in 1927 was an important pioneer effort which included fantastic drawings of the city of the future, "modernistic" skyscrapers, constructivists, robot costumes, theatre settings, and factories, together with some excellent machines and photographs of machinery.

of machines. Malyevitch, Lissitsky and Mondriaan have used technicians' tools, the compass and the square, to achieve "abstract" geometrical paintings of a machine-like precision. Picabia and Grosz used machines to invoke the mirthless laughter of dadaism.

The Russian constructivists, Tatlin, Gabo, Pevsner, employed the technique, the materials and something of the structural feeling of machinery. The severity and glittering polish of machines have also affected the sculptors Brancusi, Archipenko and Belling.

Machine art has been the principal influence which has purged the best post-war architecture from the compromises of both the "modernistic" and revivalist architects. It is true that the ideas back of Le Corbusier's famous phrase "the house should be a *machine à habiter*" have given rise to much naive and dreary functionalism. But the leaders of modern architecture today are united in restoring the artistic function of the architect to its place beside his technical function.

Machine Forms and Natural Forms.

The beauty of the machine art in so far as it is a mere by-product of function may seem a meagre and even trivial kind of beauty. But this is not necessarily so. The beauty of all natural objects is also a by-product—the helix of a snail's shell (and a steel coil), the graduated feathering of a bird's wing (and the leaves of a laminated spring), the rabbit's footprints in the snow (and the track of non-skid tires), the elegance of fruit (and of incandescent bulbs).

"Industry and Culture"

It is in part through the aesthetic appreciation of natural forms that man has carried on his spiritual conquest of nature's hostile chaos. Today man is lost in the far more treacherous wilderness of industrial and commercial civilization. On every hand machines literally multiply our difficulties and point our doom. If, to use L. P. Jack's phrase, we are to "end the divorce" between our industry and our culture we must assimilate the machine aesthetically as well as economically. Not only must we bind Frankenstein—but we must make him beautiful.

A. H. B., Jr.

HISTORY OF MACHINE ART.

Machine Art and Handicraft.

The history of machine art is interwoven with that of handicraft, but in spirit machine art and handicraft are diametrically opposed. Handicraft implies irregularity, picturesqueness, decorative value and uniqueness: figured textiles, pottery vases, decorative friezes, hand-wrought metal work, hand-hammered silver bowls. The machine implies precision, simplicity, smoothness, reproducibility: plain textiles, vases as simple as laboratory beakers, smooth polished metal work.

The difference between craft and the machine lies in spirit and convention as much as in actual method of manufacture. Tools, and simple machines have always been used: the potter's wheel and the hand loom are machines. Modern equipment is merely more efficient and complex. But whether the designer sits at the loom and works up the pattern as he weaves or whether a motor weaves and the designer sits in an office, the actual work is by machine. A man at a hand loom can weave a rug of machine-like simplicity. A glass blower can make laboratory beakers as well as picturesquely shaped vases. But the craft spirit does not fit an age geared to machine technique. Machine-made imitations of craft objects are parodies, and the real handicrafts have lost their original vigor.

In the development of the design of machines and useful objects, the nineteenth century is an anomaly. In previous periods the normal tendency had been to utilize the best technical and mechanical devices known and to design for these devices. After the invention of the potter's wheel, vase designs were logically based on its use. But in the nineteenth century technics and design were divorced. Machines made bad designs while good designs continued to be executed by primitive methods.

The twentieth century is gradually rectifying this anomaly and is returning to the more reasonable principle of designing tools and useful objects with reference to the latest technique, out of the most durable material, and as economically as possible. In the same way the mother art of architecture has achieved style after the revivals of the nineteenth century by once more fusing with the latest technique of building science.

The Nineteenth Century.

The Industrial Revolution and the development of machine production in England in the latter part of the eighteenth century brought only ugliness to ordinary life. It caused slums; it built ugly factories. For utensils it made bad replicas of ugly hand-made objects. People of sensibility in the nineteenth century hated the machines which seemed ugly and created ugliness. They failed to see the possibilities inherent in the new technics. Instead, they misused or rejected the new technics and developed their architecture and useful arts on a handicraft basis.

Nevertheless the science of engineering in the nineteenth century produced a few great buildings. The Crystal Palace at the London Exposition of 1851 is now considered one of the important ancestors of modern architecture. At the time, however, its great mass of glass and steel framework was considered too plain and ugly to deserve even the label of architecture. All the engineering works of the latter part of the nineteenth century and the beginning of the twentieth were considered mere utilitarian objects and as such were looked down upon. The science of building, however, developed rapidly and by the time of the World War had produced many excellent factories, grain silos and bridges.

Meanwhile architecture, independently of engineering, was moving toward simplicity. Philip Webb, Norman Shaw and their followers broke away from Classical and Medieval Revivalism and started the movement known as Queen Anne. In America, H. H. Richardson under the guise of Romanesque Revivalism, was creating his own sturdy simplicity. But only after the War did the stream of architecture join the stream of engineering, to give birth to a genuinely modern architecture. The development of the dependent arts paralleled that of architecture.

At first Gothic and Classical ornament (Fig. a), then Victorian rococo ornament was used whenever possible in designing machine art. Remarkable exceptions were the designs of Sir Joseph Whitworth, strictly simple and functional (Fig. b). He exhibited his machines in the same London Exposition of 1851 where the Crystal Palace caused so much comment. They received no more approbation from the designers of the day than the Crystal Palace did from the architects.

William Morris, the great reformer of the minor arts, especially hated the machine; indeed, it made him almost physically ill to look at the Crystal Palace which he visited as a young man from Oxford. His whole life was devoted to a crusade against the machine and for the ideals of art in everyday objects and art created by the common man himself.

This movement was at the time a healthy one. The minor arts on the

Continent of Europe had become sterile adaptations by indifferent craftsmen of Classical and Baroque forms. Morris had real ideas of simplicity and good workmanship which have their influence even at present. He and his followers revolutionized design in the minor arts toward simplicity and originality, although Morris himself believed that he was reviving the Gothic style.

The English Arts and Crafts Movement reached its heights in the '90s in the work of Voysey, MacIntosh and Baillie Scott, but was not acknowledged as a modern movement until it had been transplanted to the Continent, where it thrived in Vienna and Brussels under the leadership of such men as Josef Hoffmann and Henry van der Velde. Indeed one phase of the Arts and Crafts Movement on the Continent, characterized by curvilinear and naturalistic ornament, may even be called a style: the *Art Nouveau* (Fig. c).

Fig. a

Fig. b

Drill Press, pre-Civil War American. Now on display at the New York Museum of Science & Industry.

Classical architecture in machine design, typical of the mid-nineteenth century. This false art drove William Morris and his followers to the refuge of medievalistic handicraft.

Whitworth Drill Press, designed by Sir Joseph Whitworth in the middle of the nineteenth century. Now on display at the New York Museum of Science & Industry.

Straightforward machine design by the father of modern machine tool building. The aesthetic possibilities of these simple lines, entirely ignored by Whitworth's contemporaries, are only today being realized.

The Twentieth Century.

As in architecture it was only after the War that designers realized the possibility of beauty in the construction of machines. In Germany particularly the post-war generation prided itself on achieving a mechanistic age and on designing the proper utensils for living in it. This was most clearly expressed in the Bauhaus School at Weimar under the leadership of Walter Gropius. In spite of a cubist aesthetic and much left over craft spirit, the movement was more and more toward machine-like simplicity. It was here, for instance, that Marcel Breuer first developed the now ubiquitous tubular steel chair. The movement in Germany has been more and more against *Kunstgewerbe*—Arts and Crafts—until the modern expositions of what we call industrial art are practically free from that tradition.

Fig. c.

Silver Bowl, Henry van de Velde, designer, ca. 1900

An example of the curvilinear Art Nouveau at its best. This was developed on the Continent out of the English Arts and Crafts Movement. The work of designers like van de Velde was as important in the development of modern machine art as technical improvements like Whitworth's.

The situation in America has been somewhat special. The Arts and Crafts developments in Europe have affected us less, whereas the tradition of machine construction has been purer and stronger. Our precision instruments especially have led the world (Nos. 289 to 313). But our minor arts have suffered from imitation of second-hand European designs.

In 1900 Louis Tiffany was the only designer whose work was independent and known outside America. For the most part we inherited the worst of the English Arts and Crafts Movement and the worst of the Art Nouveau style, the worst of the Viennese Kunstgewerbe.

In the '20's we received a fresh wave of foreign influence from France. Though France herself was influenced from central Europe, the Paris Exposition of Decorative Arts of 1925, with its neo-classic trappings and bizarre ornament, made a strong impression on our designers. The problem in America has not been the conflict against a strong handicraft tradition but rather against a "modernistic" French machine-age aesthetic.

Besides the French Decorative movement in the '20's there developed in America a desire for "styling" objects for advertising. Styling a commercial object gives it more "eye-appeal" and therefore helps sales. Principles such as "streamlining" often receive homage out of all proportion to their applicability.

Conscious design and the development in machine building have fused and the twentieth century restores the art of making machines and useful objects to its place, as a technic of making rapidly, simply and well the useful objects of current life.

The Scope of the Exhibition.

The Exhibition contains machines, machine parts, scientific instruments and objects useful in ordinary life. There are no purely ornamental objects; the useful objects were, however, chosen for their aesthetic quality. Some will claim that usefulness is more important than beauty, or that usefulness makes an object beautiful. This Exhibition has been assembled from the point of view that though usefulness is an essential, appearance has at least as great a value.

The Exhibition cannot be exhaustive. The very number of useful objects and machines made it impossible even to cover the whole field in making the choices. Exigencies of space prohibited many large items. Inaccessibility prevented choosing items locally distributed in the Far and and Middle West. Yet the Exhibition tries to be representative. Some fields, the kitchen and the laboratory, for example, are more fully present than others. This is because the nineteenth century did not consider these objects worthy of decorative treatment.

For the convenience of the reader and the visitor to the Exhibition, the list of objects is divided according to use into six categories.

1. **Industrial units:** Machines and machine parts: springs, insulators, cable sections, propeller blades, etc.
2. **Household and office equipment:** Sink, furnace, bathroom cabinets, dishwasher, carpet sweeper and business machines.
3. **Kitchenware**
4. **House furnishings and accessories:** Objects used in daily life: tableware, vases and bowls, smoking accessories, lighting fixtures, and furniture.
5. **Scientific instruments:** Precision, optical, drafting and surveying instruments.
6. **Laboratory glass and porcelain:** Beakers, hydrometer jars, petri dishes and boiling flasks.

P. J.

SHORT LIST OF BOOKS

Historical:

Day, Lewis F.	Of William Morris and his work. London, Virtue, 1899.
Osthaus, Karl Ernst.	Van de Velde. Hagen i. W., Folkwang-Verlag, 1920. (Die neue Baukunst I)
Popp, J.	Deutsches Warenbuch, herausgegeben von der Dürerbund-Werkbund Genossenschaft. Kriegsausgabe. Munich, D.B.W.B., 1915.
Gropius, Walter.	Staatliches Bauhaus, Weimar 1919–1923 Walter Gropius and others. Weimar-Munich, Bauhausverlag, n.d.

Contemporary:

Gropius, Walter, and Moholy-Nagy, L., ed.	Neue Arbeiten der Bauhauswerkstätten. Munich, Langan 1925. (Bauhausbücher 7)
Pfleiderer, Wolfgang, introd.	Die Form ohne Ornament: Werkbundausstellung 1924. Stuttgart, Deutsche Verlags-Anstalt, 1924. (Bücher der Form I)
Le Corbusier.	L'art décoratif d'aujourd'hui. Paris, Crès, n.d.
Kollmann, Franz.	Schönheit der Technik. Munich, Langen, 1928.
Vogt, Richard.	Der neue Markt: Standardartikel aus der industriellen Produktion. Berlin, VDI-Verlag, 1931.

DIVISIONS OF THE EXHIBITION

1. **Industrial units**
2. **Household and office equipment**
3. **Kitchenware**
4. **House furnishings and accessories**
5. **Scientific instruments**
6. **Laboratory glass and porcelain**

Within each division the objects are listed according to use.

Listing of each object is as follows: Name of the object
Name of the manufacturer
Name of the designer
Price

Unless otherwise specified the object may be purchased from the manufacturer.

An asterisk before a catalog number indicates that the work is illustrated by a plate which bears the same number.

1. INDUSTRIAL UNITS

*1. Bearing spring
American Steel & Wire Co.
Subsidiary United States Steel Corp.

*2. Section of spring
American Steel & Wire Co.
Subsidiary United States Steel Corp.

3. Air brake spring
American Steel & Wire Co.
Subsidiary United States Steel Corp.

4. Railroad car spring
American Steel & Wire Co.
Subsidiary United States Steel Corp.

*5. Typewriter carriage spring
American Steel & Wire Co.
Subsidiary United States Steel Corp.

*6. Motor spring
American Steel & Wire Co.
Subsidiary United States Steel Corp.

7. Clock spring
Westinghouse Electric & Mfg. Co.

8. Bumper ring for electric refrigerator
American Steel & Wire Co.
Subsidiary United States Steel Corp.

9. Clutch spring
American Steel & Wire Co.
Subsidiary United States Steel Corp.

10. Grease cup spring
American Steel & Wire Co.
Subsidiary United States Steel Corp.

11. Fine wire spring
American Steel & Wire Co.
Subsidiary United States Steel Corp.

12. Coil of strip stainless steel
American Steel & Wire Co.
Subsidiary United States Steel Corp.

13. Steel balls for ball bearings
S K F Industries

14. Polished small steel bearings
Westinghouse Electric & Mfg. Co.

15. Carnegie beam sections
Scully Steel Products Co.
Subsidiary United States Steel Corp.

16. Standard beam sections
Scully Steel Products Co.
Subsidiary United States Steel Corp.

17. Steel T sections
Scully Steel Products Co.
Subsidiary United States Steel Corp.

18. Steel channel sections
Scully Steel Products Co.
Subsidiary United States Steel Corp.

19. Steel rail sections
Scully Steel Products Co.
Subsidiary United States Steel Corp.

20. Bare concentric strand of electrical cable
American Steel & Wire Co.
Subsidiary United States Steel Corp.

21. Bare sector strand of electrical cable
American Steel & Wire Co.
Subsidiary United States Steel Corp.

22. Hollow conductor of an electrical cable
American Steel & Wire Co.
Subsidiary United States Steel Corp.

23. Lock coil cable
American Steel & Wire Co.
Subsidiary United States Steel Corp.

24. Submarine power cable
American Steel & Wire Co.
Subsidiary United States Steel Corp.

25. Armored submarine power cable
American Steel & Wire Co.
Subsidiary United States Steel Corp.

*26. Section of wire rope $3\frac{1}{2}$″ in diameter
American Steel & Wire Co.
Subsidiary United States Steel Corp.

27. Cross-sections of unusual wire shapes
American Steel & Wire Co.
Subsidiary United States Steel Corp.

28. Ordinary rail bond
American Steel & Wire Co.
Subsidiary United States Steel Corp.

29. Third rail bond
American Steel & Wire Co.
Subsidiary United States Steel Corp.

30. Chain of rigid type insulators 12″ in diameter
Westinghouse Electric & Mfg. Co.

31. Type PN grey strain insulator
Westinghouse Electric & Mfg. Co.

32. Ball and socket suspension insulator
Westinghouse Electric & Mfg. Co.

33. Apparatus type insulator
Westinghouse Electric & Mfg. Co.

34. Porcelain wall bushing
Westinghouse Electric & Mfg. Co.

35. Apparatus type insulator valve
Westinghouse Electric & Mfg. Co.

INDUSTRIAL UNITS—*Continued*

36. Steel car wheel with axle and rail
 Carnegie Steel Co.
 Subsidiary United States Steel Corp.

37. Rectangular, oval and streamlined tubes of aluminum
 Aluminum Company of America

38. Stainless steel tubing sections
 National Tube Company
 Subsidiary United States Steel Corp.

39. Large boat propeller, iron
 Sullivan Shipyards, Inc.

40. Boat propeller, bronze
 Electric Boat Co.

*41. Outboard propeller
 Aluminum Company of America

42. Aeroplane propeller
 Hamilton-Standard Propeller Corp.
 Rough forged blades, Aluminum Company of America

43. Radiator tubes with aluminum fins
 Aluminum Company of America

44. Arco convector
 American Radiator Co.

45. Murray radiator
 American Radiator Co.

46. Steel gears
 Atlantic Gear Works

47. Stainless steel wing rib for aeroplane, shot-welded
 Fleetwings, Inc.

48. Automobile hub cap
 American Sheet & Tin Plate Co.
 Subsidiary United States Steel Corp.

49. Automobile pistons
 Aluminum Company of America

*50. Self-aligning ball bearing
 S K F Industries

51. Automobile headlamps
 Ford Motor Co.

52. Circular wood-cutting cross-cut saw
 Henry Disston & Sons, Inc.

53. Plastering trowel, stainless steel
 Henry Disston & Sons, Inc.

*54. Gasoline pump
 Standard Oil Co. of Ohio

55. Welded ball of Enduro stainless steel
 Sholes Inc., New York

56. Switchboard
 Westinghouse Electric & Mfg. Co.
 Lent by Clyde-Mallory Line

2. HOUSEHOLD AND OFFICE EQUIPMENT

*57. Lavatory panel of the Arco Panel Unit System, equipped with special tubular fittings
 The Accessories Co., Inc. Division of American Radiator Co.
 George Sakier, designer
 Panel: $60.00; Standard Sanitary lavatory: $50.00. Licensed plumbers

58. Special medicine cabinet with sliding mirror door
 The Accessories Co., Inc. Division of American Radiator Co.
 George Sakier, designer
 $75.00

59. Recess supply cabinet
 Conant Bros. Co.
 $140.00

60. Mirror
 Conant Bros. Co.
 $19.00

*61. Niedecken mixer faucet
 Hoffmann & Billings Mfg. Co.
 $25.00. Henry Stein, 50 Cliff St., N. Y.

*62. Flush valve
 Scovill Mfg. Co. Plumbers' Brass Goods Division
 Licensed plumbers

*63. Electrol-Kewanee heating unit, model 10
 Electrol Inc.
 Gerth & Gerth, designers
 $857.00

*64. Electrochef range, model B-2
 Electromaster Inc., Detroit, Michigan
 Emil Piron, designer
 $110.00

*65. Streamline Monel metal sink
 The International Nickel Co., Inc.
 Gustav Jensen, designer
 $193.50. Licensed plumbers

HOUSEHOLD AND OFFICE EQUIPMENT—*Continued*

*66. Electric plate warmer, White House Line
Janes & Kirtland, Inc.
$100.00.   Department stores

67. Thermotainer, roll warmer
Waters-Genter Co.   Division of McGraw
Electric Co.
$385.00.   Tumbridge Sales Corp., New
York

68. Broom closet, White House Line, Small
House model
Janes & Kirtland, Inc.
$33.75.   Department stores

69. Cupboard and drawer base unit with Monel
metal counter
Janes & Kirtland, Inc.
$33.85.   Department stores

70. Exhaust fan
Westinghouse Electric & Mfg. Co.
Department and hardware stores

*71. Fay electric floor machine, Diamond model
The Fay Co.
$65.00.   Department, furniture and hard-
ware stores

*72. Hamilton Beach vacuum cleaner, model 8
Hamilton Beach Mfg. Co.   Subsidiary
Scovill Mfg. Co.
$34.75.   Department, furniture and hard-
ware stores

*73. Silver Streak carpet sweeper
Bissell Carpet Sweeper Co.
$5.00.   Department, furniture and hard-
ware stores

74. The Conover electric dishwasher
The Conover Co.
$160.00.   Department stores

*75. Health scale number 711
Hanson Scale Co.
$12.95.   Department and hardware stores

*76. Toastmaster, automatic electric toaster
Waters-Genter Co.   Division of McGraw
Electric Co.
$85.00.   Tumbridge Sales Corp., N. Y.

*77. Wafflemaster, automatic electric waffle
baker
Waters-Genter Co.   Division of McGraw
Electric Co.
$85.00.   Tumbridge Sales Corp., N. Y.

*78. Range, BG-1, with 4 glass coffee machines
The Silex Co.
$56.95.   E. B. Latham & Co., New York

79. Teaket
The Silex Co.
$1.25.   Department and hardware stores

80. Cafex
The Silex Co.
$2.95.   Department and hardware stores

*81. Door knob and lock
P. & F. Corbin
Howe & Lescaze, designers
$14.75

82. Door knob and lock
P. & F. Corbin
$15.00

83. Loose joint hinges
P. & F. Corbin
$4.50 a pair

84. Olive hinges
P. & F. Corbin
$8.15 a pair

*85. Yale Junior Lock
Yale & Towne Mfg. Co.
60¢.   Hardware stores

*87. Dictaphone, model 12
Dictaphone Corp.
Stanford Briggs, designer
$200.00

*88. National cash register, model 1934
The National Cash Register Co.
$325.00

89. Tulip drinking cup dispenser, equipped with
aluminum tube for airplane, railroad
and steamship service
Lily-Tulip Cup Corp.
$3.00

90. Tulip soda cup dispenser
Lily-Tulip Cup Corp.
$6.85

*91. York round door chest, model 480
York Safe and Lock Co.

92. Grain of wheat lamp
Westinghouse Electric & Mfg. Co.

93. Automobile tail-light lamp
Westinghouse Electric & Mfg. Co.

94. Automobile head-light lamp
Westinghouse Electric & Mfg. Co.

95. 10 W. 5-11 lamp
Westinghouse Electric & Mfg. Co.

96. 100 W. 7-8 lamp
Westinghouse Electric & Mfg. Co.

HOUSEHOLD AND OFFICE EQUIPMENT—*Continued*

97. 300 W. T-10 lamp
Westinghouse Electric & Mfg. Co.

98. 500 W. T-20 lamp
Westinghouse Electric & Mfg. Co.

99. 250 W. G-30 lamp
Westinghouse Electric & Mfg. Co.

100. 1000 W. G-40 lamp
Westinghouse Electric & Mfg. Co.

101. 5000 W. bipost base lamp
Westinghouse Electric & Mfg. Co.

102. 10,000 W. lamp
Westinghouse Electric & Mfg. Co.

3. KITCHENWARE

105. Wear-Ever steam jacketed kettle
The Aluminum Cooking Utensil Co.
$236.00

106. Stock pot, Staybrite nonoxyd metalware
L. D. Cahn Co.
$17.00

107. Stock pots, rustless steel
Polar Ware Co.
$36.00 to $50.00

108. Wear-Ever stock pots
The Aluminum Cooking Utensil Co.
$6.50 to $12.15

109. Bain Marie pots, rustless steel
Polar Ware Co.
$2.30 to $6.60

110. Hotel pan, rustless steel
Polar Ware Co.
$5.10

111. Wear-Ever hotel sauté pans
The Aluminum Cooking Utensil Co.
$3.30 to $7.45

112. Crusader hotel sauce pans
Lalance & Grosjean Mfg. Co.
$6.70 to $25.00

*113. Crusader hotel sauce pots
Lalance & Grosjean Mfg. Co.
$14.55 to $31.65

114. Sauce pan, Staybrite nonoxyd metalware
L. D. Cahn Co.
$10.00

115. Coffee urn cylinder, Staybrite nonoxyd metalware
L. C. Cahn Co.
$27.00

116. Coffee urn cup, rustless steel
Polar Ware Co.
$6.00

*117. Crusader hotel ladles
Lalance & Grosjean Mfg. Co.
$1.08 to $4.45

118. Wear-Ever bakers' mixing bowl
The Aluminum Cooking Utensil Co.
$4.85

*119. Crusader bakers' bowls
Lalance & Grosjean Mfg. Co.
$25.00 to $64.75

*120. Wear-Ever food containers
The Aluminum Cooking Utensil Co.
93¢ to $3.55.   Department stores

121. Wear-Ever food bowls
The Aluminum Cooking Utensil Co.
50¢ to 65¢.   Department stores

122. Crusader pail
Lalance & Grosjean Mfg. Co.
$12.53.   Department stores

123. Crusader malted milk shaker
Lalance & Grosjean Mfg. Co.
$4.15.   Department stores

124. Solid ladle, Staybrite nonoxyd metalware
L. D. Cahn Co.
$2.25

125. Dipper
Polar Ware Co.
$7.50

126. Apple cup
Polar Ware Co.
$1.60

127. Frying pans
Polar Ware Co.
$5.00 and $6.00

128. Frying pan, Staybrite nonoxyd metalware
L. D. Cahn Co.
$4.25

KITCHENWARE—*Continued*

129. French fryers
     Revere Copper & Brass Inc.   Rome
     Manufacturing Division
     $1.80 and $2.00.   Department stores

130. Skillet
     Revere Copper & Brass Inc.   Rome
     Manufacturing Division
     $2.00.   Department stores

*131. Stewpans, black enamel
     Imported by Markt & Hammacher
     75¢ to $1.35.   Lewis & Conger

*132. Saucepans
     Revere Copper & Brass Inc.   Rome
     Manufacturing Division
     $1.80 to $2.20.   Department stores

133. Mixing bowls, black enamel
     Imported by Markt & Hammacher
     $2.15.   Lewis & Conger

134. Mixing bowls
     Polar Ware Co.
     $3.00 to $8.00

*135. Mixing bowls
     Revere Copper & Brass Inc.   Rome
     Manufacturing Division
     90¢ to $1.30.   Department stores

136. Crusader cup
     Lalance & Grosjean Mfg. Co.
     $1.84.   Department stores

*137. Wear-Ever round cake pans
     The Aluminum Cooking Utensil Co.
     30¢ to 45¢.   Department stores

138. Wear-Ever ring cake mold
     The Aluminum Cooking Utensil Co.
     $1.00.   Department stores

139. Wear-Ever fruit press
     The Aluminum Cooking Utensil Co.
     93¢.   Department stores

140. Wear-Ever tea kettle
     The Aluminum Cooking Utensil Co.
     Lurelle V. A. Guild, designer
     $2.95.   Department stores

141. Wear-Ever drip coffee pot
     The Aluminum Cooking Utensil Co.
     Lurelle V. A. Guild, designer
     $1.65.   Department stores

*142. Wear-Ever griddle
     The Aluminum Cooking Utensil Co.
     $3.95.   Department stores

*143. Beverage tumblers, rustless steel
     Polar Ware Co.
     90¢

*144. Bathroom tumblers, rustless steel
     Polar Ware Co.
     $1.75

*145. Imported cook's knives
     Lent by Lewis & Conger
     $2.34 and $3.25

*146. Imported cook's fork
     Lent by Lewis & Conger
     $1.88

*147. Imported slicers
     Lent by Lewis & Conger
     $2.00 to $4.50

148. Square coffee jars
     Owens-Illinois Glass Co.

*149. Nestrite paper containers
     Lily-Tulip Cup Corp.

150. Nestrite paper tubs
     Lily-Tulip Cup Corp.

*151. Squat Nestrite containers
     Lily-Tulip Cup Corp.

Hospital Supplies

*152. Needle box, rustless steel
     Polar Ware Co.
     $3.70

153. Serum cup
     The Aluminum Cooking Utensil Co.
     20¢

154. Sputum cup with hinged cover, Staybrite
          nonoxyd metalware
     L. D. Cahn Co.
     $3.00

*155. Graduated measure, Staybrite nonoxyd
          metalware
     L. D. Cahn Co.
     $5.50

156. Sponge bowl, rustless steel
     Polar Ware Co.
     $2.00

4. HOUSE FURNISHINGS AND ACCESSORIES

157. Dinner knives, Covington Plain pattern
The Gorham Co.
A reproduction of an old English design by
W. C. Codman
$41.00 per dozen.   Silversmiths and department stores

158. Dinner forks, Covington Plain pattern
The Gorham Co.
A reproduction of an old English design
by W. C. Codman
$50.00 per dozen.   Silversmiths and department stores

159. Teaspoons, Covington Plain pattern
The Gorham Co.
A reproduction of an old English design
by W. C. Codman
$21.00 per dozen.   Silversmiths and department stores

*160. Dessert spoons, Covington Plain pattern
The Gorham Co.
A reproduction of an old English design
by W. C. Codman
$37.00 per dozen.   Silversmiths and department stores

*161. Dessert knives, Covington Plain pattern
The Gorham Co.
A reproduction of an old English design by
W. C. Codman
$37.00 per dozen.   Silversmiths and department stores

*162. Dessert forks, Covington Plain pattern
The Gorham Co.
A reproduction of an old English design
by W. C. Codman
$35.00 per dozen.   Silversmiths and department stores

163. Coffee spoons, Covington Plain pattern
The Gorham Co.
A reproduction of an old English design
by W. C. Codman
$14.00 per dozen.   Silversmiths and department stores

164. Dinner knives, Dolly Madison pattern
The Gorham Co.
Original early American design by A. H. Staf
$49.00 per dozen.   Silversmiths and department stores

165. Dinner forks, Dolly Madison pattern
The Gorham Co.
Original early American design by A. H. Staf
$52.00 per dozen.   Silversmiths and department stores

166. Teaspoons, Dolly Madison pattern
The Gorham Co.
Original early American design by A. H. Staf
$21.00 per dozen.   Silversmiths and department stores

*167. Dessert spoons, Dolly Madison pattern
The Gorham Co.
Original early American design by A. H. Staf
$46.00 per dozen.   Silversmiths and department stores

168. Dessert knives, Dolly Madison pattern
The Gorham Co.
Original early American design by A. H. Staf
$39.00 per dozen.   Silversmiths and department stores

*169. Dessert forks, Dolly Madison pattern
The Gorham Co.
Original early American design by A. H. Staf
$44.00 per dozen.   Silversmiths and department stores

170. Coffee spoons, Dolly Madison pattern
The Gorham Co.
Original early American design by A. H. Staf
$12.00 per dozen.   Silversmiths and department stores

*171. Windsor teaspoons, chromium
Lent by Lewis & Conger
25¢ each

*172. Windsor dessert spoons, chromium
Lent by Lewis & Conger
42¢ each

*173. Windsor table spoons, chromium
Lent by Lewis & Conger
48¢ each

174. Crystal bread and butter plate
Fostoria Glass Co.
$4.00 per dozen.   Department stores and gift shops

175. Crystal salad plate
Fostoria Glass Co.
$5.00 per dozen.   Department stores and gift shops

176. Crystal dinner plate
Fostoria Glass Co.
$7.00 per dozen.   Department stores and gift shops

177. Crystal service plate
     Fostoria Glass Co.
     $15.00 per dozen. Department stores and
     gift shops

*178. White porcelain bread and butter plate
     Lenox Inc.
     $13.25 per dozen. Department stores and
     gift shops

*179. White porcelain luncheon plate
     Lenox Inc.
     $16.00 per dozen. Department stores and
     gift shops

*180. White porcelain dinner plate
     Lenox Inc.
     $19.00 per dozen. Department stores and
     gift shops

*181. White porcelain service plate
     Lenox Inc.
     $21.00 per dozen. Department stores and
     gift shops

182. White porcelain sandwich or cake plate
     Lenox Inc.
     $3.50. Department stores and gift shops

183. Tumblers, crystal with sham bottoms
     Fostoria Glass Co.
     $3.50 per dozen. Department stores and
     gift shops

184. Tumblers, crystal with sham bottoms
     Fostoria Glass Co.
     $4.50 per dozen. Department stores and
     gift shops

*185. Tumblers, blue glass
     Fostoria Glass Co.
     $2.50 per dozen. Department stores and
     gift shops

*186. Tumblers, burgundy glass
     Fostoria Glass Co.
     $2.50 per dozen. Department stores and
     gift shops

187. Liqueur tumblers, crystal with sham bot-
     toms
     Fostoria Glass Co.
     $2.00 per dozen. Department stores and
     gift shops

188. Cocktail glass
     Corning Glass Works—Steuben Division
     Walter Dorwin Teague, designer
     $2.00 each. Steuben Glass, Inc., 748 Fifth
     Avenue

189. Old-Fashioned cocktail glass
     Corning Glass Works—Steuben Division
     Walter Dorwin Teague, designer
     $2.00 each. Steuben Glass, Inc., 748 Fifth
     Avenue

190. Whisky glasses
     Fostoria Glass Co.
     $3.50 per dozen. Department stores and
     gift shops

191. Baccarat ale glass
     Lent by Lewis & Conger
     $8.50 per dozen

192. Baccarat ale glass
     Lent by Lewis & Conger
     $10.00 per dozen

193. Baccarat champagne tumbler
     Lent by Lewis & Conger
     $5.50 per dozen

194. Baccarat claret glass
     Lent by Lewis & Conger
     $9.75 per dozen

195. Baccarat cocktail glass
     Lent by Lewis & Conger
     $9.75 per dozen

196. Baccarat cordial glass
     Lent by Lewis & Conger
     $8.75 per dozen

197. Baccarat goblet
     Lent by Lewis & Conger
     $14.75 per dozen

198. Baccarat sherry glass
     Lent by Lewis & Conger
     $10.50 per dozen

199. Baccarat tumbler
     Lent by Lewis & Conger
     $7.50 per dozen

200. Baccarat whisky glass
     Lent by Lewis & Conger
     $5.50 per dozen

201. Baccarat whisky and soda glass
     Lent by Lewis & Conger
     $6.25 per dozen

202. Holland glass brandy inhalers
     Lent by Ovington's
     $18.00 per dozen

203. Cocktail glasses
     Lent by Ovington's

204. Tumblers
     Lent by Ovington's

205. Martini mixer
     Lent by Carol Stupell
     $3.50

HOUSE FURNISHINGS AND ACCESSORIES—*Continued*

206. Condiment bottles
Russel Wright Studio
Russel Wright, designer
$2.00 each. Department stores and gift shops

*207. Salad bowl, wood
Russel Wright Studio
Russel Wright, designer
$3.30 each. Department stores and gift shops

*208. Berry bowl, wood
Russel Wright Studio
Russel Wright, designer
$3.00 each. Department stores and gift shops

*209. Small berry bowls, wood
Russel Wright Studio
Russel Wright, designer
$1.60 each. Department stores and gift shops

210. Baccarat fingerbowl and plate
Lent by Lewis & Conger
$33.00 per dozen

*211. Cream jars
Owens-Illinois Glass Co.

*213. Oblong perfume bottles
Owens-Illinois Glass Co.

*214. Taper round bottles
Owens-Illinois Glass Co.

*215. Jar with cover
Owens-Illinois Glass Co.

216. Wide-mouthed French squares
Owens-Illinois Glass Co.

217. Chromium tray
The Bingham Stamping & Tool Co.
$1.75. R. Aberli Jr., 225 Fifth Avenue

218. Copper tray
The Bingham Stamping & Tool Co.
$1.50. R. Aberli Jr., 225 Fifth Avenue

219. Serving tray, chromium
Chase Brass & Copper Co., Inc. Specialty Sales Division
$6.00. Department stores and gift shops

220. Serving trays, copper
Chase Brass & Copper Co., Inc. Specialty Sales Division
$6.00. Department stores and gift shops

*221. Tray, chromium
Chase Brass & Copper Co., Inc. Specialty Sales Division
Walter Von Nessen, designer
$4.00. Department stores and gift shops

222. Tray, copper
Chase Brass & Copper Co., Inc. Specialty Sales Division
Walter Von Nessen, designer
$4.00. Department stores and gift shops

*223. Flower bowl, copper
Chase Brass & Copper Co., Inc. Specialty Sales Division
Walter Von Nessen, designer
$8.00. Department stores and gift shops

224. Pretzel bowl, copper
Chase Brass & Copper Co., Inc. Specialty Sales Division
$2.00. Department stores and gift shops

*225. Pretzel bowl, chromium
Chase Brass & Copper Co., Inc. Specialty Sales Division
$2.00. Department stores and gift shops

226. Bowl
Corning Glass Works—Steuben Division
Frederick Carder, designer
$6.00. Steuben Glass, Inc., 748 Fifth Ave.

*227. Bowl
Corning Glass Works—Steuben Division
Walter Dorwin Teague, designer
Steuben Glass, Inc., 748 Fifth Avenue

*228. Bowl
Corning Glass Works—Steuben Division
Walter Dorwin Teague, designer
$4.25. Steuben Glass, Inc., 748 Fifth Avenue

229. Large crystal plate, 16″ diameter
Fostoria Glass Co.
$3.50. Department stores and gift shops

230. Bowl, wood
Russel Wright Studio
Russel Wright, designer
$5.00. Department stores and gift shops

231. Copper bowls
Revere Copper & Brass Inc., Rome Mfg. Division
50¢ and 75¢. Department stores and gift shops

*232. White porcelain vases
Lenox Inc.
$1.50, $2.50, $3.00. Department stores and gift shops

233. Crystal vases
Fostoria Glass Co.
$2.50 and $3.00. Department stores and gift shops

234. Vase, square
Corning Glass Works—Steuben Division
Frederick Carder, designer
$3.50. Steuben Glass, Inc., 748 Fifth Ave.

*235. Vase, spherical
Corning Glass Works—Steuben Division
Walter Dorwin Teague, designer
$8.50. Steuben Glass, Inc., 748 Fifth Ave.

236. Vase, rectangular
Corning Glass Works—Steuben Division
Walter Dorwin Teague, designer
$5.00. Steuben Glass, Inc., 748 Fifth Ave.

*237. Vases
Corning Glass Works—Steuben Division
Walter Dorwin Teague, designer
$2.75 to $3.75. Steuben Glass, Inc., 748
Fifth Avenue

*238. Black glass vases
Corning Glass Works—Steuben Division
Walter Dorwin Teague, designer
$2.75 to $3.75. Steuben Glass, Inc.,
748 Fifth Avenue

239. Plates, chromium and copper
Chase Brass & Copper Co., Inc. Specialty
Sales Division
Department stores and gift shops

240. Centerpiece
Corning Glass Works—Steuben Division
Walter Dorwin Teague, designer
$30.00. Steuben Glass, Inc., 748 Fifth
Avenue

*241. Ash tray
Lent by Arundell Clarke Ltd.
$2.50

*242. Ash tray
Corning Glass Works—Steuben Division
Frederick Carder, designer
$7.50. Steuben Glass, Inc., 748 Fifth Ave.

*243. Ash tray set
Fostoria Glass Co.
$6.00 per dozen. Department stores and
gift shops

244. Ash bowl, stainless steel
Platinel Inc.
$9.50

245. Ash tray, copper
Revere Copper & Brass Inc. Rome Mfg.
Division
25¢. Department stores and gift shops

246. Ash tray, chromium
Kurt Versen
$1.60

247. Dunhill's Bruyère straight grain pipe
Alfred Dunhill of London, Inc.
$50.00. Dunhill shops, tobacco shops and
department stores

*248. Meerschaum pipe
Alfred Dunhill of London, Inc.
$25.00. Dunhill shops, tobacco shops and
department stores

*249. Tall wafer cigarette lighter
Alfred Dunhill of London, Inc.
$10.00. Dunhill shops, tobacco shops and
department stores

250. Giant cigarette lighter
Alfred Dunhill of London, Inc.
$15.00. Dunhill shops, tobacco shops and
department stores

*251. Ball cigarette lighter
Alfred Dunhill of London, Inc.
$15.00. Dunhill shops, tobacco shops and
department stores

252. Cigar case
Alfred Dunhill of London, Inc.
$22.50. Dunhill shops, tobacco shops and
department stores

*253. Bomb Rumidor
Distillers Products Corp.
$7.00. Department stores and tobacco
shops

*254. Lektrolite cigarette lighter, Cylinda model
"B", sterling silver
Platinum Products Co.
$12.00. Department stores and gift shops

*255. Lektrolite cigarette lighter and pencil, ster-
ling silver
Platinum Products Co.
$25.00. Department stores and gift shops

*256. Cigarette box
Corning Glass Works—Steuben Division
Frederick Carder, designer
$4.50. Steuben Glass, Inc., 748 Fifth Ave.

*257. Inkstand and calendar
I. S. Pertofsky
Howe & Lescaze, designers
$32.00. Howe & Lescaze, architects

258. Braquette picture frame, portrait type
Design Engineers, Inc.
Nathan George Horwitt, designer
$2.50. Eastman Kodak stores

259. Braquette picture frame, standard type
Design Engineers, Inc.
Nathan George Horwitt, designer
$2.00. Eastman Kodak stores

HOUSE FURNISHINGS AND ACCESSORIES—*Continued*

260. Bomb flashlight
Chase Brass & Copper Co., Inc. Specialty Sales Division
$1.00. Department stores and gift shops

265. Luxmir Shaving Mirror
Lent by Ovington's
$12.50

*266. Imported chromium scent bottles in leather case
Lent by Saks-Fifth Avenue
$7.50

267. Man's fitted case
Lent by Saks-Fifth Avenue
$6.50

*268. Billiard balls
Lent by Saks-Fifth Avenue
$7.50

*269. Silverice (for chilling drinks)
Lent by Saks-Fifth Avenue
$2.50 for box of six

*270. Electric clock
Herman Miller Clock Co.
Gilbert Rohde, designer
$16.50. Department stores and gift shops

*271. Westclox handbag watch, bakelite case
Western Clock Co.
De Vaulchier & Blow, designers
$2.95. Department stores, gift shops, drug stores

*272. Magnetric clock
Jaeger Watch Co.
Jaeger Watch Co., designers, in collaboration with the Art and Color section of the Fisher Body Corp. for General Motors

*273. Desk lamp
Kurt Versen
Howe & Lescaze, designers
$31.00

274. Ceiling fixture with white opal glass bowl
Kurt Versen
$14.00

275. Pendant sphere lighting fixtures
Kurt Versen
$15.00 to $34.00

*276. Tubular wall bracket
Kurt Versen
$22.00

*277. Wall bracket light with cylindrical bowl
Kurt Versen
$17.00

278. Wall bracket light with hemispherical bowl
Kurt Versen
$19.00

*279. Chair
Thonet Bros., Inc.
Marcel Breuer, designer
$20.50

*280. Chair
Thonet Bros., Inc.
Le Corbusier, designer
$63.00

*281. Nest tables
Thonet Bros., Inc.
$28.50

*282. Beta chair
The Howell Co. (Brown & Nightingale, New York distributors)
Nathan George Horwitt, designer
$30.00. Department and furniture stores

283. Chair, number 444
The Howell Co. (Brown & Nightingale, New York distributors)
$40.00. Department and furniture stores

284. Lounge chair, number 439
The Howell Co. (Brown & Nightingale, New York distributors)
$50.00. Department and furniture stores

285. Chair, number 477
The Howell Co. (Brown & Nightingale, New York distributors)
$30.00. Department and furniture stores

286. Chair, number 441
The Howell Co. (Brown & Nightingale, New York distributors)
$20.00. Department and furniture stores

5. SCIENTIFIC INSTRUMENTS

288. Johansson third measuring instrument, used
in 1898
Ford Motor Co. (Standard Gage Co.)
Louis C. Eitzen Co., New York

*289. Vernier depth gauge number 600
Brown & Sharpe of New York, Inc.
$16.25.   Hardware stores

290. Rule depth gauge number 616
Brown & Sharpe of New York, Inc.
$2.00.   Hardware stores

*291. Graduated rod depth gauge number 614
Brown & Sharpe of New York, Inc.
$4.50.   Hardware stores

*292. Plain English micrometer number 8
Brown & Sharpe of New York, Inc.
$9.50.   Hardware stores

*293. Inside micrometer number 263
Brown & Sharpe of New York, Inc.
$7.50.   Hardware stores

*294. Outside firm joint caliper number 821
Brown & Sharpe of New York, Inc.
60 cents.   Hardware stores

*295. Caliper square with adjusting screw number
560
Brown & Sharpe of New York, Inc.
$10.20.   Hardware stores'

296. Caliper rule number 391
Brown & Sharpe of New York, Inc.
$5.00.   Hardware stores

297. Slide caliper rule number 385
Brown & Sharpe of New York, Inc.
$2.50.   Hardware stores

298. Pocket slide caliper rule number 388
Brown & Sharpe of New York, Inc.
$4.00.   Hardware stores

299. Flexible stainless steel rule number 356
Brown & Sharpe of New York, Inc.
$1.35.   Hardware stores

300. Narrow tempered steel rule number 303
Brown & Sharpe of New York, Inc.
90¢.   Hardware stores

301. Rule with slide number 380
Brown & Sharpe of New York, Inc.
$2.00.   Hardware stores

302. Hardened and ground steel parallel number
920
Brown & Sharpe of New York, Inc.
$1.00.   Hardware stores

303. Hardened steel straight edge number 527
Brown & Sharpe of New York, Inc.
$1.00.   Hardware stores

304. Hardened cast steel try squares number 540
Brown & Sharpe of New York, Inc.
$3.60 to $34.50.   Hardware stores

305. Adjustable square complete number 554
Brown & Sharpe of New York, Inc.
$4.20.   Hardware stores

306. Graduated steel square number 544
Brown & Sharpe of New York, Inc.
$3.90.   Hardware stores

*307. Diemakers' square complete number 552
Brown & Sharpe of New York, Inc.
$5.50.   Hardware stores

308. Indicator number 738
Brown & Sharpe of New York, Inc.
$10.00.   Hardware stores

309. Speed indicator number 748
Brown & Sharpe of New York, Inc.
$6.75.   Hardware stores

*310. Vest pocket speed indicator number 746
Brown & Sharpe of New York, Inc.
$1.50.   Hardware stores

*311. 29 degrees worm thread tool gauge number
577
Brown & Sharpe of New York, Inc.
$7.50.   Hardware stores

312. Dial gauge number 726
Brown & Sharpe of New York, Inc.
$10.00.   Hardware stores

*313. Bevel protractor number 493
Brown & Sharpe of New York, Inc.
$10.50.   Hardware stores

*314. Laboratory microscope ESA-105
Carl Zeiss, Inc.
$159.00

315. Research microscope, model L
Carl Zeiss, Inc.
$573.80 (with objectives)

316. Binocular microscope XB
Carl Zeiss, Inc.
$183.05

317. Iris cylinder diaphragm
Carl Zeiss, Inc.
$6.50

318. Abbe apertometer
Carl Zeiss, Inc.
$52.00

SCIENTIFIC INSTRUMENTS—*Continued*

319. Short magnifier lamp
Carl Zeiss, Inc.
$13.15

320. Plankton vessel
Carl Zeiss, Inc.
$2.00

321. Simplified attachable mechanical stage
Carl Zeiss, Inc.
$18.00

322. Ramsden screw micrometer
Carl Zeiss, Inc.
$44.00

323. Focusing microscope for photo-engravers
Carl Zeiss, Inc.
$55.00

324. Folding aplanatic magnifiers
Carl Zeiss, Inc.
$8.15 each

325. Aplanatic magnifiers
Carl Zeiss, Inc.
$6.90 each; lens ring and handle, $1.90

*326. Diaphot
Carl Zeiss, Inc.
$2.20

327. Stereoscope
Carl Zeiss, Inc.
$40.00

328. Vertical telescope view finder (for Contax camera)
Carl Zeiss, Inc.
$15.40

*329. Telescope, 80 mm.
Carl Zeiss, Inc.
$1,166.25

330. Hand spectroscope, model A
Carl Zeiss, Inc.
$18.00

*331. Cube of didymium glass
Carl Zeiss, Inc.
$5.00

332. Blood sugar colorimeter
Carl Zeiss, Inc.
$27.50

*333. Sugar and oil refractometer
Carl Zeiss, Inc.
$211.20

334. Pulfrich refractometer
Carl Zeiss, Inc.
$458.40

*335. Juerst ebulliometer
Eimer & Amend
$75.00

*336. MacMichael viscosimeter
Eimer & Amend
$210.00

337. Small vertex refractionometer
Carl Zeiss, Inc.
$115.00

338. Demonstration attachment for cystoscopes
Carl Zeiss, Inc.
$90.00

339. Polarimeter with circular scale
Carl Zeiss, Inc.
$186.25

*340. Pocket polarimeter
Carl Zeiss, Inc.
$83.25

341. Triple mirror for light signals
Carl Zeiss, Inc.

342. Prism
Holophane Co.

343. Controlenses
Holophane Co.

*344. Adjustable curve number 2160
Eugene Dietzgen Co., Inc.
$2.25

*345. Adjustable curve number 2161 A
Eugene Dietzgen Co., Inc.
$2.65

346. Wood blackboard outfit: arc, protractor, T-square, and triangle
Eugene Dietzgen Co., Inc.
$5.70

*347. Protractor, nickel silver
Eugene Dietzgen Co., Inc.
$41.80

*348. Protractor, steel
Eugene Dietzgen Co., Inc.
$10.00

349. Slide rule
Eugene Dietzgen Co., Inc.
$10.55

*350. Pocket sight compass
Eugene Dietzgen Co., Inc.
$8.35

*351. Short & Mason miner's compass
Taylor Instrument Companies
$40.00. Department, optical and hardware stores

SCIENTIFIC INSTRUMENTS—*Continued*

*352. Brass plumb bob
Eugene Dietzgen Co., Inc.
$1.90

353. Mercury plumb bob number 790
Brown & Sharpe of New York, Inc.
$3.60.   Hardware stores

354. DX Projection type ammeter
Westinghouse Electric & Mfg. Co.

355. DX Projection type rectox voltmeter
Westinghouse Electric & Mfg. Co.

356. PY-5 a.c. portable voltmeter
Westinghouse Electric & Mfg. Co.

357. Stroboscopic clock motor testing board
Westinghouse Electric & Mfg. Co.

358. Light meter
Westinghouse Electric & Mfg. Co.

*359. Dental instruments
The S. S. White Dental Mfg. Co.

*360. Dietometer
Eimer & Amend
$9.00

*361. Torsion prescription scale number 285
The Torsion Balance Co.
$80.00

362. Micromax recording potentiometer
Leeds & Northrup Co., Philadelphia
$250.00

363. Brown indicating flowmeter number 2020
The Brown Instrument Co., Philadelphia
$108.75

364. Altitude barometer
Taylor Instrument Companies
$42.00.   Department, optical and hardware stores

*365. Anemometer
Taylor Instrument Companies
$50.00.   Department, optical and hardware stores

*366 X-ray unit, model "B", stationary type
Ritter Dental Mfg. Co., Inc.
$820.00

6. LABORATORY GLASS AND PORCELAIN

*367. Crystallizing dishes
Corning Glass Works
45¢ to $1.25.   Eimer & Amend

*368. Boiling flasks
Corning Glass Works
57¢ to $3.30.   Eimer & Amend

369. Boiling flasks with wicker necks
Corning Glass Works
$1.35 and $1.55.   Eimer & Amend

370. Erlemeyer flasks
Corning Glass Works
38¢ to $1.60.   Eimer & Amend

371. Beakers
Corning Glass Works
18¢ to 50¢.   Eimer & Amend

*372. Reagent bottles
Corning Glass Works
65¢ to $3.00.   Eimer & Amend

373. Cylindrical jars
Corning Glass Works
$1.20 to $10.00.   Eimer & Amend

*374. Hydrometer jars
Eimer & Amend
40¢ to $2.75

*375. Battery jars
Eimer & Amend
$4.70 to $13.25

376. Battery jars
Corning Glass Works
$1.15 to $2.60.   Eimer & Amend

*377. Petri dishes
Eimer & Amend
24¢ to 70¢

378. Moist chambers
Eimer & Amend
$1.40 and $1.80

*379. Stender dishes
Eimer & Amend
50c. to $2.00

380. Flask 500 cc
Eimer & Amend
$1.85

*381. Measuring flask
Eimer & Amend
$1.60

382. Measuring cylinder 500 cc
Eimer & Amend
$4.25

383. Weighing bottles
Eimer & Amend
30¢ to $1.60

384. Shaking flask
Eimer & Amend
$1.20

385. B jar
Eimer & Amend
$8.00

386. Bell jar and frame
Eimer & Amend
$16.00

387. Generating bottle
Eimer & Amend
$2.35

388. Culture flask
Corning Glass Works
65¢.   Eimer & Amend

389. Roux culture flask
Corning Glass Works
65¢.   Eimer & Amend

390. Round bottom boiling flask, 72 litres
Corning Glass Works
$25.00.   Eimer & Amend

391. Solution bottle
Corning Glass Works
$4.00.   Eimer & Amend

392. Watch glass
Eimer & Amend
60¢

*393. Scorifiers
Eimer & Amend
60¢

*394. Retort
Corning Glass Works
$3.60.   Eimer & Amend

*395. Capsules
Coors Porcelain Co.
15¢ to 25¢.   Eimer & Amend

396. Rings
Coors Porcelain Co.
$9.95.   Eimer & Amend

LABORATORY GLASS AND PORCELAIN—*Continued*

*397. Dish
    Coors Porcelain Co.
    $1.60.   Eimer & Amend

*398. Beakers
    Coors Porcelain Co.
    55¢ to $9.00.   Eimer & Amend

399. Petri covers
    Coors Porcelain Co.
    15¢ and 20¢.   Eimer & Amend

400. Jar
    Coors Porcelain Co.
    $129.00.   Eimer & Amend

401. Sample oil bottles
    Owens-Illinois Glass Co.

402. Jar and cover
    Eimer & Amend
    $2.25

1. Industrial Units

Illustrations

1

Bearing spring

American Steel & Wire Co.
Subsidiary United States Steel Corp.

2

Section of spring

American Steel & Wire Co.
Subsidiary United States Steel Corp.

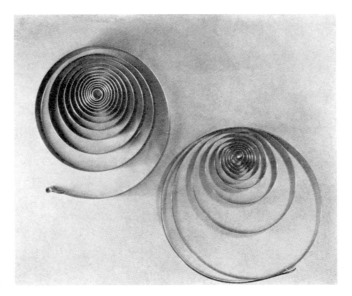

5, 6

Typewriter carriage spring and motor spring

American Steel & Wire Co.
Subsidiary United States Steel Corp.

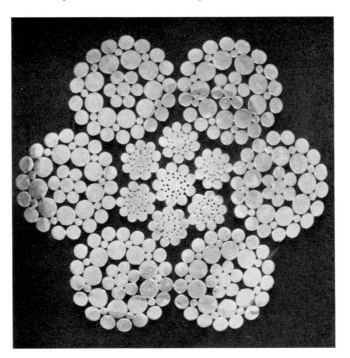

26

Section of wire rope $3\frac{1}{2}''$ in diameter

American Steel & Wire Co.
Subsidiary United States Steel Corp.

50

Self-aligning ball bearing
S K F Industries

41

Outboard propeller
Aluminum Company of America

54

Gasoline pumps
Standard Oil Company of Ohio

2. Household and Office Equipment

Illustrations

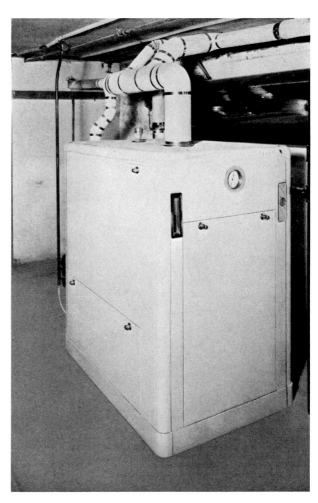

63

Electrol-Kewanee heating unit, model 10

Electrol, Inc.

Gerth & Gerth, designers

$857.00

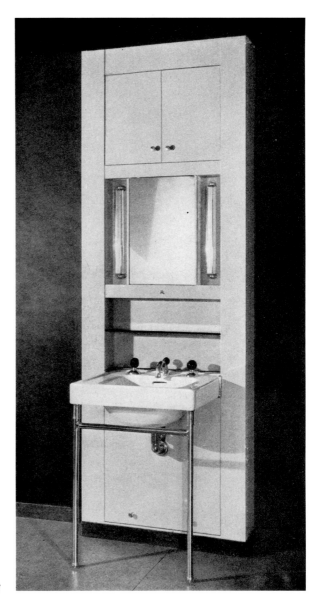

57

Lavatory panel of the Arco panel unit system, equipped with special tubular fittings

The Accessories Co., Inc.
Division of American Radiator Co.

George Sakier, designer

Panel: $60.00; Standard Sanitary lavatory: $50.00. Licensed plumbers

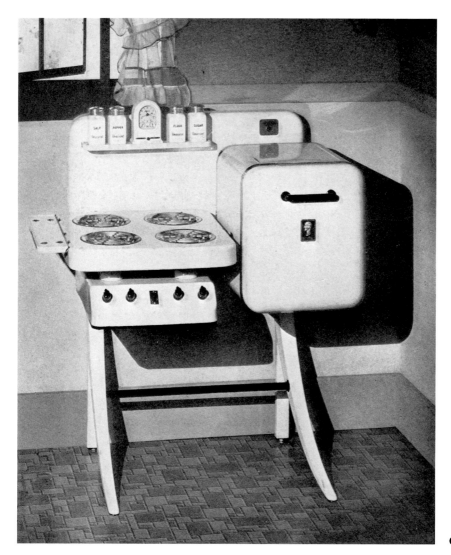

64

Electrochef range, model B-2

Electromaster Inc., Detroit, Michigan

Emil Piron, designer

$110.00

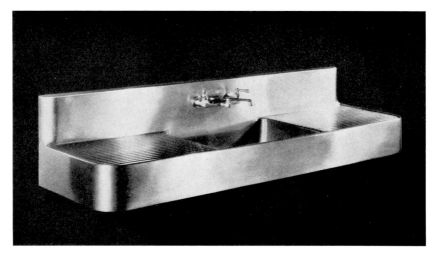

65

Streamline Monel metal sink
The International Nickel Co., Inc.
Gustav Jensen, designer
$193.50.   Licensed plumbers

66

Electric plate warmer, White House Line
Janes & Kirtland, Inc.
$100.00.   Department stores

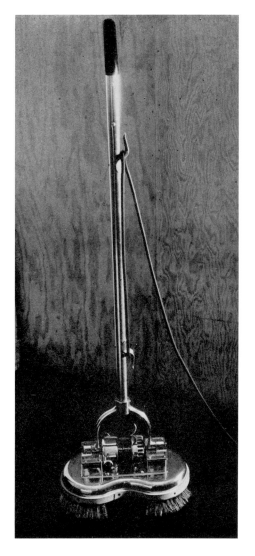

71

Fay electric floor machine, Diamond model

The Fay Co.

$65.00. Department, furniture and hardware stores

72

Hamilton Beach vacuum cleaner, model 8

Hamilton Beach Mfg. Co.
Subsidiary Scovill Mfg. Co.

$34.75. Department, furniture and hardware stores

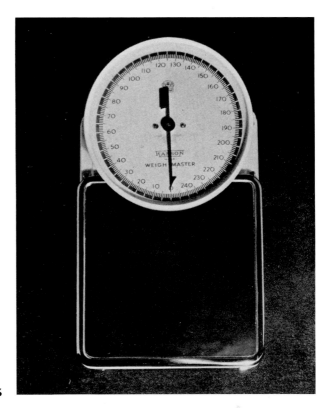

75

Health scale, number 711

Hanson Scale Co.

$12.95.   Department and hardware stores

73

Silver Streak carpet sweeper

Bissell Carpet Sweeper Co.

$5.00.   Department, furniture and hardware stores

62

Flush valve

Scovill Mfg. Co.
Plumbers' Brass Goods Division

Licensed plumbers

61

Niedecken mixer faucet
Hoffmann & Billings Mfg. Co.
$25.00 Henry Stein, 50 Cliff St.

77

Wafflemaster, automatic electric waffle baker

Waters-Genter Co.
Division of McGraw Electric Co.

$85.00.   Tumbridge Sales Corp.

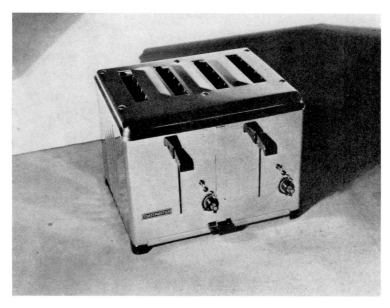

76

Toastmaster, automatic electric toaster

Waters-Genter Co.
Division of McGraw Electric Co.

$85.00.   Tumbridge Sales Corp.

87

Dictaphone, model 12
Dictaphone Corp.
$200.00.   Dictaphone Sales Corp.

88

National Cash Register, model 1934
The National Cash Register Co.
$325.00

91

York round door chest, model 480
York Safe and Lock Co.

85

Yale junior lock
Yale & Towne Mfg. Co.
60¢. Hardware stores

78

Range with 4 glass coffee machines
The Silex Co.
$56.95.   E. B. Latham & Co.

81

Door knob and lock
P. & F. Corbin
Howe & Lescaze, designers
$14.75

3. Kitchenware

Illustrations

113

Crusader hotel sauce pots
Lalance & Grosjean Mfg. Co.
$14.55 to $31.65.

117

Crusader hotel ladles
Lalance & Grosjean Mfg. Co.
$1.08 to $4.45

119

Crusader bakers' bowl
Lalance & Grosjean Mfg. Co.
$25.00 to $64.75

131

Stewpans

Imported by Markt & Hammacher

75¢ to $1.35.   Lewis & Conger

135

Mixing bowls

Revere Copper & Brass
Inc.
Rome Mfg. Division

90¢ to $1.30.
Department stores

155

Graduated measures, Staybrite nonoxyd metalware

L. D. Cahn Co.

132

Saucepan

Revere Copper & Brass Inc.
Rome Mfg. Division

$1.80 to $2.20. Department stores

143
144

Beverage and bathroom tumblers, rustless steel
Polar Ware Co.
90¢ and $1.65

149
151

Nestrite paper con-
tainers

Lily-Tulip Cup Corp.

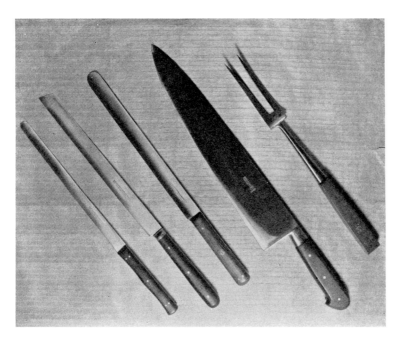

145, 147

Imported cooks' knives and slicers
Lewis & Conger
$2.00 to $4.50

146

Imported cooks' fork
Lewis & Conger
$1.88

152

Needle box, rustless steel
Polar Ware Co.
$3.70

137

Wear-Ever round cake
pans

The Aluminum
Cooking Utensil Co.

30¢ to 50¢
Department stores

140

Wear-Ever tea kettle

The Aluminum
Cooking Utensil Co.

Lurelle V. A. Guild,
designer

$2.95.   Department
stores

120

Wear-Ever food containers
The Aluminum Cooking Utensil Co.
93¢ to $3.55.   Department stores

142

Wear-Ever griddle
The Aluminum Cooking Utensil Co.
$3.95.   Department stores

4. House Furnishings and Accessories

Illustrations

160-162

Dessert spoons, knives and forks, Covington Plain pattern
The Gorham Co.
A reproduction of an old English design by W. C. Codman
Spoons and knives, $37.00 per dozen; forks, $35.00 per dozen
Silversmiths and department stores

167, 169

Dessert spoons and forks, Dolly Madison pattern

The Gorham Co.

Original early American design by A. H. Staf

Spoons, $46.00 per dozen; forks, $44.00 per dozen

Silversmiths and department stores

185, 186

Tumblers, Burgundy and blue glass
Fostoria Glass Co.
$2.50 per dozen.   Department stores and gift shops

171-173

Windsor chromium teaspoons, dessert spoons and table spoons
Lent by Lewis & Conger
25¢, 42¢ and 48¢ each

215

Jar with cover
Owens-Illinois Glass Co.

213

Oblong perfume bottles
Owens–Illinois Glass Co.

211, 214

Cream jars and taper round bottles
Owens–Illinois Glass Co.

237

Vases

Corning Glass Works—Steuben Division

Walter Dorwin Teague, designer

$2.75 to $3.75.   Steuben Glass, Inc., 748 Fifth Avenue

238

Black glass vases

Corning Glass Works—Steuben Division

Walter Dorwin Teague, designer

$2.75 to $3.75.   Steuben Glass, Inc., 748 Fifth Avenue

178-181

White porcelain plates

Lenox Inc.

$13.25 to $21.00 per dozen.   Department stores and gift shops

232

White porcelain vase

Lenox Inc.

$3.00.   Department stores and gift shops

225

Pretzel bowl, chromium

Chase Brass & Copper Co., Inc. Specialty Sales Division

$2.00. Department stores and gift shops

223

Flower bowl, copper

Chase Brass & Copper Co., Inc. Specialty Sales Division

Walter Von Nessen, designer

$8.00. Department stores and gift shops

221

Serving tray, chromium
Chase Brass & Copper Co., Inc. Specialty Sales Division
Walter Von Nessen, designer
$4.00. Department stores and gift shops

235

Spherical vase
Corning Glass Works—Steuben Division
Walter Dorwin Teague, designer
$8.50. Steuben Glass, Inc., 748 5th Ave.

207-209

Wood salad bowl, berry bowl and small berry bowls

Russel Wright Studio
Russel Wright, designer

Salad bowl, $3.30; berry bowl, $3.00; small bowls, $1.60 each
Department stores and gift shops

228

Bowl

Corning Glass Works—Steuben Division

Walter Dorwin Teague, designer

$4.25.   Steuben Glass, Inc., 748 Fifth Avenue

227

Bowl

Corning Glass Works—Steuben Division

Walter Dorwin Teague, designer

$42.00 (with octagonal mirror base)

269

Silverice (for chilling drinks)

Lent by Saks-Fifth Avenue

$2.50 for box of six

268

Billiard balls

Lent by Saks-Fifth Avenue

$7.50 in leather box

257

Inkstand and calendar

I. S. Pertofsky

Howe & Lescaze, designers

$32.00.   Howe & Lescaze, architects

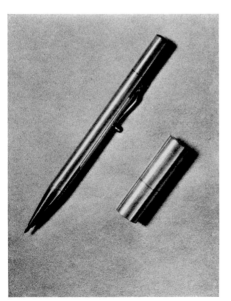

254, 255

Lektrolite Cylinda lighter and Lektrolite pencil lighter, sterling silver

Platinum Products Co.

Cylinda lighter, $12.00; pencil, $25.00. Department stores and gift shops

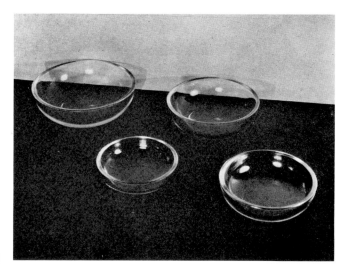

243

Ash tray set

Fostoria Glass Co.

$6.00 per dozen.   Department stores and gift shops

241

Ash tray

Lent by Arundell Clarke, Ltd.

$2.50

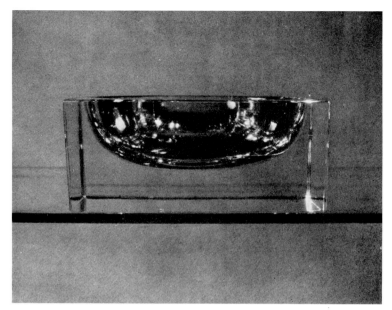

242

Ash tray

Corning Glass Works—
Steuben Division

Frederick Carder,
designer

$7.50. Steuben Glass,
Inc., 748 Fifth Avenue

256

Cigarette box

Corning Glass Works—
Steuben Division

Frederick Carder,
designer

$4.50. Steuben Glass,
Inc., 748 Fifth Avenue

248

Meerschaum pipe

Alfred Dunhill of London, Inc.
$25.00. Dunhill shops, tobacco shops and department stores

253

Bomb Rumidor

Distillers Products Corp.
$7.00. Department stores and tobacco shops

249
251

Tall wafer lighter and ball lighter
Alfred Dunhill of London, Inc.
Wafer lighter, $10.00; ball lighter, $15.00
Dunhill shops, tobacco shops and department stores

266

Imported chromium scent bottles
Lent by Saks-Fifth Avenue
$7.50 in black leather case

270

Electric clock

Herman Miller Clock Co.

Gilbert Rohde, designer

$16.50.   Department stores and gift shops

272

Magnetric clock

Jaeger Watch Co.

Jaeger Watch Co., designers, in collaboration with the Art and Color Section of the Fisher Body Corp. for General Motors

271

Westclox handbag watch, bakelite case
Western Clock Co.

De Vaulchier & Blow, designers

$2.95.   Department stores, gift shops, drug stores

Hi Williams

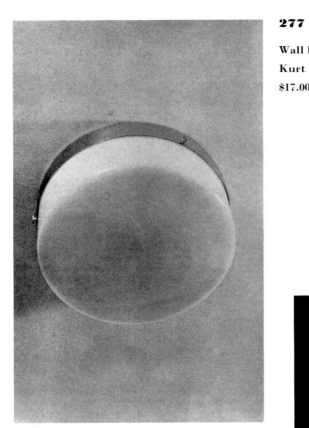

277

Wall bracket with cylindrical bowl
Kurt Versen
$17.00

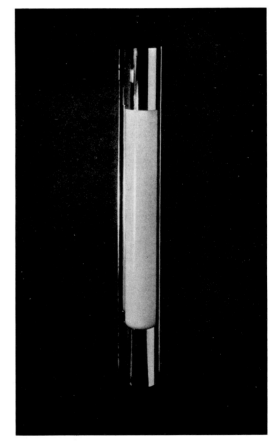

276

Tubular wall bracket
Kurt Versen
$22.00

273

Desk lamp
Kurt Versen
Howe & Lescaze, designers
$31.00

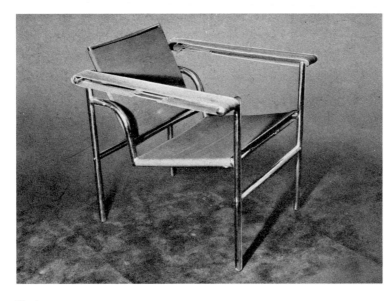

280

Chair
Thonet Bros., Inc.
Le Corbusier, designer
$63.00

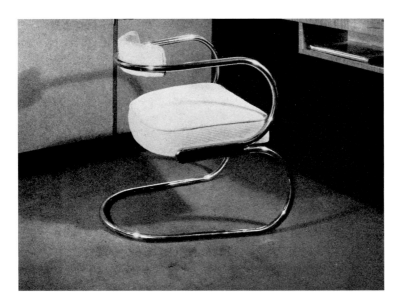

282

Beta chair
The Howell Co. (Brown & Nightingale, New York distributors)
Nathan George Horwitt, designer
$30.00.   Department and furniture stores

281

Nest tables
Thonet Bros., Inc.
$28.50

279

Chair
Thonet Bros., Inc.
Marcel Breuer, designer
$20.50

5. Scientific Instruments

Illustrations

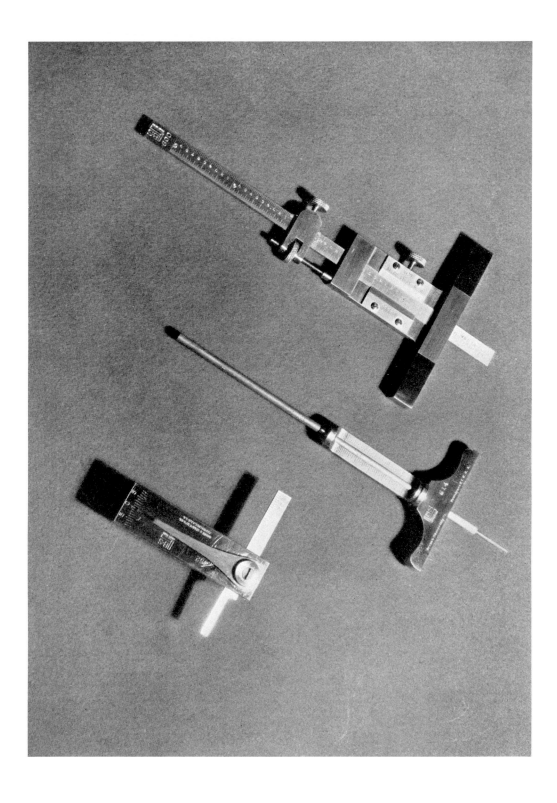

293

Inside micrometer
For taking internal measurements from 1 to 2 inches

Brown & Sharpe of New York, Inc.

$7.50.   Hardware stores

←

289

Vernier depth gauge
For measuring depth with aid of vernier scale to 1/1000 inch

Brown & Sharpe of New York, Inc.

$16.25.   Hardware stores

291

Graduated rod depth gauge for measuring depth of holes

Brown & Sharpe of New York, Inc.

$4.50.   Hardware stores

307

Diemakers' square
For checking included angle of clearance in making dies

Brown & Sharpe of New York, Inc.

$5.50.   Hardware stores

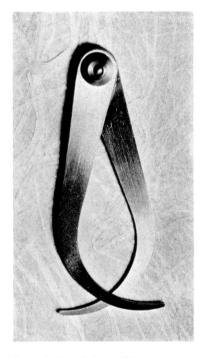

294

Outside firm joint caliper
For obtaining outside measurements (used in connection with scale)

Brown & Sharpe of New York, Inc.

60¢.   Hardware stores

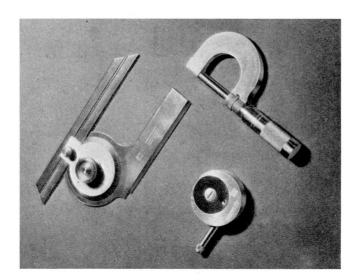

313

Bevel protractor
For obtaining angle of bevel
in actual material
Brown & Sharpe of New
York, Inc.
$10.50.   Hardware stores

292

Plain English micrometer
For measuring thickness, etc.
of steel to 1/1000 inch
Brown & Sharpe of New
York, Inc.
$9.50.   Hardware stores

310

Vest pocket speed indicator
To indicate speed of lathes,
shafts of motors, etc.
Brown & Sharpe of New
York, Inc.
$1.50.   Hardware stores

295

Caliper square with adjusting
screw

For obtaining inside and outside
measurements to 1/64 and 1/100
inch

Brown & Sharpe of New York,
Inc.

$10.20.   Hardware stores

311

29 degrees worm thread tool
gauge

For checking angles of helical
threads

Brown & Sharpe of New York,
Inc.

$7.50.   Hardware stores

340

Pocket Polarimeter
For ascertaining the concentration of sugar
solutions and solutions of optically active
substances

Carl Zeiss, Inc.

$83.25

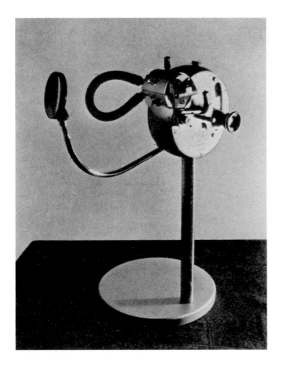

333

Sugar and oil refractometer
For measuring the refractive index and the
dispersion of liquids as well as solids

Carl Zeiss, Inc.

$211.20

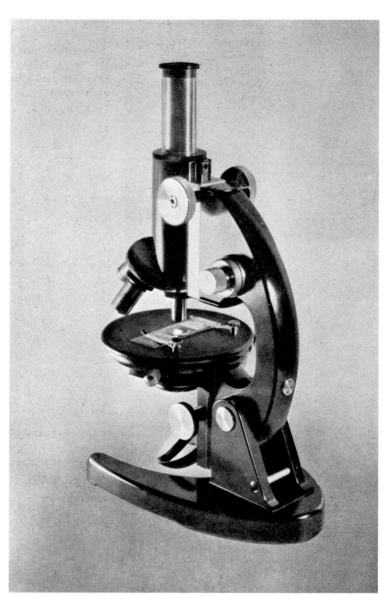

314

Laboratory microscope ESA-105

Carl Zeiss, Inc.

$159.00

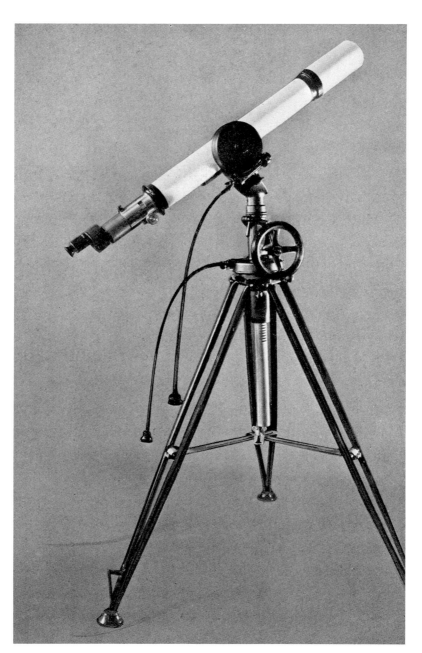

329

Telescope, 80 mm
Carl Zeiss, Inc.
$1,166.25

326

Diaphot
Exposure indicator for photographers

Carl Zeiss, Inc.

$2.20

331

Cube of didymium glass
For demonstrating with a spectroscope the sharp absorption bands characteristic of didymium salts

Carl Zeiss, Inc.

$5.00

350

Pocket sight compass

Eugene Dietzgen Co., Inc.

$8.35

351

Short & Mason miner's compass
To indicate direction of ore

Taylor Instrument Companies

$40.00.   Department, optical and hardware
stores

348

Protractor

Eugene Dietzgen Co., Inc.

$10.00

347

Protractor

Eugene Dietzgen Co., Inc.

$41.80

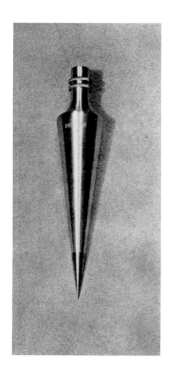

352

Brass plumb bob
Eugene Dietzgen Co., Inc.
$1.90

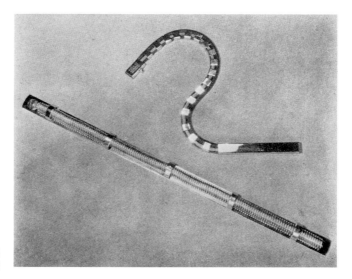

344
345

Adjustable curve number 2160
Eugene Dietzgen Co., Inc.
$2.25

Adjustable curve number 2161 A
Eugene Dietzgen Co., Inc.
$2.65

335

Juerst ebulliometer
For ascertaining the alcoholic content
of beverages

Eimer & Amend

$75.00

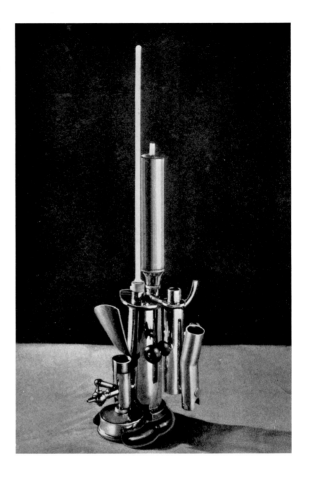

360

Dietometer
For obtaining the weight of
food in preparing diets

Eimer & Amend

$9.00

336

MacMichael viscosimeter
For ascertaining the viscosity of fluids

Eimer & Amend

$210.00

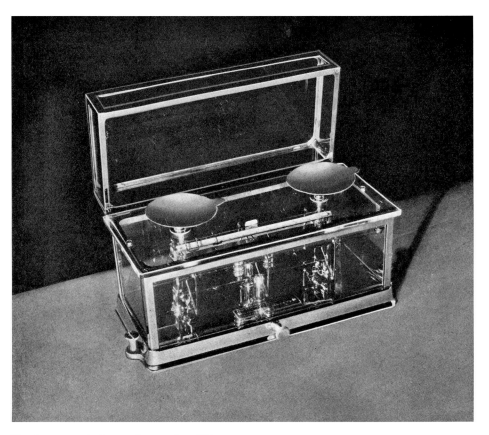

361

Torsion prescription scale number 285
The Torsion Balance Co.
$80.00

365

Anemometer
For measuring air speeds

Taylor Instrument Companies

$50.00.   Department, optical and hardware stores

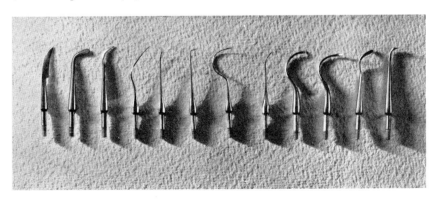

359

Dental instruments
The S. S. White Dental Mfg. Co.

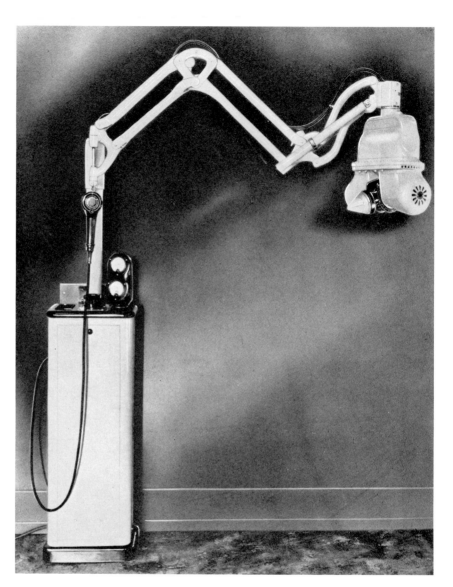

366

X-ray unit, model "B", stationary type
Ritter Dental Mfg. Co., Inc.
$820.00

6. Laboratory Glass and Porcelain

Illustrations

381

Measuring flask
Eimer & Amend
$1.60

368

Boiling flasks

Corning Glass Works

57¢ to $3.30.   Eimer & Amend

379

Stender dishes

Eimer & Amend

50¢ to $2.00

374

Hydrometer jars

Footed cylinders used to float hydrometer, an instrument which indicates the specific gravity of a solution

Eimer & Amend

40¢ to $2.75

377

Petri dishes
Used in growing cultures
Eimer & Amend
24¢ to 70¢

367

Crystallizing dishes
Used in obtaining crystals from saturated solutions by evaporation
Corning Glass Works
45¢ to $1.25.   Eimer & Amend

372

Reagent bottles
Corning Glass Works
65¢ to $3.00.   Eimer & Amend

393

Scorifiers
Used in assay-
ing the metal-
lic content of
ores

Eimer &
Amend

60¢

394

Retort
Used in distilling liquids

Corning Glass Works

$3.60.   Eimer & Amend

375

Battery jars
Used in making storage
batteries

Eimer & Amend

$4.70 to $13.25

398

Beakers
Used for dissolving, drying or boiling solutions
Coors Porcelain Co.
55¢ to $9.00.   Eimer & Amend

395

Capsules
Used for drying or incinerating chemicals
Coors Porcelain Co.
15¢ to 25¢.   Eimer & Amend

397

Dish
Coors Porcelain Co.
$1.60.   Eimer & Amend

MUSEUM PUBLICATIONS

The books published by the Museum of Modern Art in connection with its numerous exhibitions form a concise library of living art, painting, sculpture, and architecture. The critical and historical notes, explanations by the artists, biographies and bibliographies contain information not readily found elsewhere. There is a wealth of illustration—over 893 plates of the work of over 300 modern painters, sculptors and architects. The Museum makes no profit on these books. It sells them considerably below the cost of production, as a part of its educational service to students and the public.

Nineteenth Century Painters and Sculptors

Cezanne, Gauguin, Seurat, van Gogh. The four great pioneers of modern painting. Critical and biographical studies by Alfred H. Barr, Jr. 152 pages; 97 plates; paper bound—$2.00

Homer, Ryder, Eakins. Essays by Bryson Burroughs, Frank Jewett Mather, and Lloyd Goodrich on these American "old masters." 68 pages; 34 plates; paper bound—$2.00

Corot and Daumier. Two painters much admired by living artists. Introduction by Alfred H. Barr, Jr. 128 pages; 108 plates; paper bound—$2.00

Toulouse-Lautrec and Odilon Redon. Introduction by Jere Abbott. Notes on artists, actors, and singers of Lautrec's circle by Daniel Catton Rich. 72 pages; 39 plates; paper bound—$2.00

The Bliss Collection. Memorial Exhibition. Out of print

American Folk Art. Most comprehensive survey so far published about American folk art, including sculpture. 28-page introduction by Holger Cahill. Bibliography of 86 books and periodicals. 131 pages; 80 plates; paper bound—$1.50; bound in boards —$3.50

Twentieth Century Painters and Sculptors

Painting in Paris. Foreword and critical notes by Alfred H. Barr, Jr. A succinct introduction to the work of the most influential school of living artists. 88 pages; 50 plates; paper bound—$2.00

Paintings by 19 Living Americans. This and the following catalog are anthologies of work by the best known contemporary American artists. Biographical notes by Alfred H. Barr, Jr. 88 pages; 38 plates; paper bound—$2.00

Painting and Sculpture by Living Americans. 67 pages; 34 plates; paper bound—$1.50

German Painting and Sculpture. Work of the leading German artists, with foreword and extensive notes by Alfred H. Barr, Jr. 91 pages; 49 plates; paper bound—$2.00

Lehmbruck and Maillol. Out of print

Murals by American Painters and Photographers. Essays by Lincoln Kirstein and Julien Levy. 62 pages; 61 plates; paper bound—$.50

American Painting and Sculpture, 1862–1932. A selection from American painting and sculpture, divided about equally between 19th and 20th century works. Introduction by Holger Cahill. 128 pages; 79 plates; paper bound—$1.50; bound in boards—$3.50

American Sources of Modern Art. Introduction on the art of ancient America and its relationship to the art of today by Holger Cahill. Bibliography of over 100 titles. 104 pages; 56 plates; paper bound—$1.50; bound in boards—$3.50

Painting and Sculpture from Sixteen American Cities. Contemporary work by 119 artists, with biographies. Edited by Alfred H. Barr, Jr. 61 pages; 116 illustrations; paper bound—$1.00; bound in boards—$2.50

Monographs on Individual Artists

Henri-Matisse. "Notes of a Painter" by Henri-Matisse; the only publication in English of these important observations. Critical essay by Alfred H. Barr, Jr. 128 pages; 82 plates; paper bound—$2.00; bound in boards—$3.00

Charles Burchfield, Early Watercolors. Foreword by Alfred H. Barr, Jr. and notes by the artist. 24 pages; 10 plates; paper bound—$1.00

Paul Klee. Out of print

Diego Rivera. Out of print

Max Weber, Retrospective Exhibition. Work by one of the most important American modernists. Foreword by Alfred H. Barr, Jr., and notes by the artist. 40 pages; 16 plates; paper bound—$1.00

Maurice Sterne. Introduction by Horace Kallen and notes by the artist. Biography by Holger Cahill. 52 pages; 23 plates; bound in boards—$2.50

Edward Hopper. "Notes on Painting" by Edward Hopper. Essays by Charles Burchfield and Alfred H. Barr, Jr. 81 pages; 48 plates; paper bound, $1.00; bound in boards, $2.50

Architecture

Modern Architecture. Introduction by Alfred H. Barr, Jr. Nine short monographs, and lists by Henry-Russell Hitchcock, Jr., and Philip Johnson. An essay on the housing problem by Lewis Mumford. Complete bibliographies. 200 pages; 65 plates; paper bound—$1.50; bound in boards—Out of print

Theatre

Theatre Art. Four centuries of Theatre Art. Edited and with introduction by Lee Simonson. Contributions by John Anderson, Paul Alfred Merbach, Oliver M. Sayler, John Mason Brown. 146 pages; 76 plates—$1.50; cloth bound—$2.00

Rivera Portfolio

Diego Rivera—A Portfolio of Color Reproductions of Mexican Frescoes. Notes by Jere Abbott. These are the first color reproductions published of the famous frescoes in Chapingo, Cuernavaca and Mexico City. Contains 19 full-color plates and 15 monotones—$25.00

Twenty-five hundred copies of this catalog were printed for the trustees of the Museum of Modern Art, New York, by the Blanchard Press, Inc., New York, March, Nineteen Thirty-four.